BOEING

12.

BOEING
757 & 767
THE MEDIUM TWINS

ROBBIE SHAW

EDITOR'S NOTE

To make the Osprey Civil Aircraft series as authoritative as possible, the editor would be interested in hearing from any individual who may have relevant information relating to the aircraft/operators featured in this, or any other, volume published by Osprey Aviation. Similarly, comments on the editorial content of this book would also be most welcome. Please write to Tony Holmes at 10 Prospect Road, Sevenoaks, Kent, TN13 3UA, Great Britain, or e-mail tony.holmes@osprey-jets.freeserve.co.uk

ACKNOWLEDGEMENT

Again I would like to thank my wife Eileen for her thankless task in proof reading.

FRONT COVER *An American Airlines (AA) B767-300(ER) climbs out of Gatwick, bound for Dallas/Fort Worth - one of the two daily flights undertaken by the airline on this route. AA has also used the MD-11 and, since March 1999, the Boeing 777 on this service.*

BACK COVER *British Airways (BA) was the joint launch customer for the B757, and the airline is the largest operator of the type outside the USA. Since taking delivery of an initial batch of 24 aircraft, the airline has steadily increased its fleet to 51. A further six are on order, although it is quite possible that due to a downturn in passenger numbers some of these might be deferred. Photographed departing Gatwick in the airline's old livery is B757-236 G-BPEE Robert Louis Stevenson. This extended range (ER) variant was originally allocated the registration G-BMRK, although the aircraft was immediately taken on charge by then BA subsidiary Caledonian Airways, who operated it as G-BPEE Loch Tay. After some seven months with Caledonian, the aircraft was returned to BA and, for several years, operated transatlantic services from Birmingham and Glasgow*

TITLE PAGE *The narrow fuselage and sleek lines of the B757 are evident in this shot of British Airways example G-CPER*

RIGHT *This shot of All Nippon 767-381(ER) JA8323, seen about to land at Osaka/Kansai airport, is dominated by the bridge in the background which links the new airport to the mainland. This aircraft is one of two operated by subsidiary Air Nippon, whose ANK logo can be seen on the nose*

First published in Great Britain in 1999 by Osprey Publishing,
Elms Court, Chapel Way, Botley, Oxford, OX2 9LP

ISBN 1 85532 903 4

Edited by Tony Holmes
Page design by Paul Kime
Cutaway Drawings by Mike Badrocke
Origination by Grasmere Digital Imaging, Leeds, UK
Printed in Hong Kong

For a catalogue of all titles published by Osprey Military, Aviation and Automotive please write to:

Osprey Direct UK, P.O. Box 140, Wellingborough, Northants NN8 4ZA, UK
E-mail: info@OspreyDirect.co.uk

Osprey Direct USA, P.O. Box 130, Sterling Heights, MI 48311-0130, USA
E-mail: info@OspreyDirectUSA.com

Or visit our website:
http://www.osprey-publishing.co.uk

Contents

LEFT *German charter B767 operator LTU - Lufftransport Unternehmen has its main bases at Dusseldorf and Munich. Operating a predominantly Boeing fleet of B757s and B767s to a variety of holiday destinations, the airline has utilised this striking scheme (seen here on B767-3G5(ER) D-AMUR) for a number of years now*

Introduction

Ever since its entry into jet airliner production with Model 707, the Boeing Company has followed one success with another. For example, having completed the production of the 1832nd, and last, Boeing 727, the tri-jet entered the record books as the world's most successful jetliner. It was only a matter of time, however, before that mantle was passed on to its 'baby brother', the B737. The introduction of the Next Generation 737 family (the series -600 to -900) has helped the 737 family to amass over 4000 orders, some 3100 of which have been delivered to date.

Aside form the B737, two other Boeing twin-jets have also been selling well for the company since making their service debuts in the early 1980s. The B757 and B767 have consistently enjoyed good 'market penetration' across the globe, and with the impending introduction of larger variants, both types should ensure continued production for many years to come. Both aircraft are capable of – and are equally at home on – either short-haul/high-density or long-haul routes. Due to this flexibility, quite a number of airlines operate both models. Indeed, the fact that both have common flight decks, which permit the two-man crew to have a common rating, and therefore fly both types, offers an added bonus – this both cuts costs on training and significantly eases crewing rosters.

The proposal to build both models was announced by Boeing in 1978. The B757 was designed as a replacement for the B727 in the short/medium range role, although it could also operate transatlantic services, both scheduled and high-density charter flights. Thanks to its range, it has become a favourite with many US operators on their transcontinental routes. Similarly, the wide-bodied B767 has also found its primary market in North America flying domestic routes. However, thanks to its configuration, the aircraft is also 'a natural' for those international routes which cannot support larger aircraft like the B747. Boeing's newest product, the B777, has, to a certain extent, taken over this mantle, which makes it rather surprising that the company has introduced the larger B767-400(ER), which effectively competes against the newer 'twin'..

Successful as they are, the B757 and B767 are now fighting a rearguard action against Airbus, and its A321 and A330, with the latter in particular racking up significant orders over the past 12 months in this traditionally Boeing market. Despite the increased competition, I am certain that both Boeing types will, early into the new millennium, each record their 1000th order – a significant achievement.

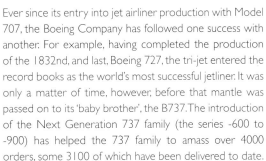

OPPOSITE TOP *Like the B757, Boeing's 767 has proven popular with the 'majors' in the USA. And as with the smaller 'twin', Delta Air Lines leads the field with 95 series -200/-300s in service, and 21 -400(ER)s on order. Again, like the B757, American Airlines is number two in the 'league table', with All Nippon Airways in third position. Displaying Delta's new livery at Gatwick in November 1998 is 767-3P6(ER) N156DL. Built in 1991, this aircraft was one of six acquired from original owner Gulf Air in 1997*

OPPOSITE BOTTOM *The Boeing 757 has proved an extremely popular aircraft for the major US airlines, thanks mainly to its capability of flying transcontinental routes. The three largest B757 operators fit into this category, and all of them operate almost 100 of the type apiece. As mentioned in the previous caption, Delta Air Lines currently has the biggest B757 fleet, but only just. In 1999 it has 99 examples in service, with a further 19 on order, which will make Delta the undisputed leader. Due to its location on the West Coast, Los Angeles' LAX is a primary destination for the B757, and Delta's N630DL is seen on short finals to the airport in October 1996*

Chapter 1

BOEING 757

The concept of the B757 can be traced to the early 1970s, when Boeing realised it needed a successor to the then highly successful B727-200. The proposed B727-300 evoked a lukewarm response from the airlines, however, and the manufacturer returned to the drawing board to think again. It then emerged with the proposed B7N7, a 160-180 seater featuring a wider fuselage cross-section and redesigned wing with two pod-mounted engines, although retaining the 'T' tail of the B727.

This time the response from potential customers was more positive, although there was criticism of the increased fuselage cross-section, particularly from airlines already operating the B727. The designers returned to their drawing boards again, and came up with the optimum solution. The cross-section of the B727 was married to the new wing and engines, while the 'T' tail was dispensed with in favour of a traditional shaped, but larger, vertical fin. Thus the B757 was born.

The long, narrow, fuselage featured six-abreast seating, with a single aisle, and capacity ranging from around 180 up to a maximum of 239 in a high-density configuration. With a range of up to 4000 nm, the aircraft could, if necessary, service transatlantic routes as well as coast-to-coast US services. The project was formally announced in February 1978 and, powered by two Rolls-Royce RB211-535C engines, it became the first Boeing airliner launched with non-US powerplants. The Pratt & Whitney PW2037 and PW2040 were certified for use at a later date, giving customers a choice of powerplant.

The first variant of the aircraft was the series -200, and launch orders were placed by Eastern Airlines and British Airways for 21 and 19 aircraft, with options on 24 and 18 more, respectively.

Major assembly of all B757s has been performed alongside B737s at Boeing's Renton plant in the south-eastern suburbs of Seattle. However, unlike the latter aircraft, most B757s receive their customer livery at Renton, which means that once an aircraft takes off from this site on its maiden flight, it seldom returns to its place of manufacture, instead landing at Boeing Field, some five miles away. Here, the aircraft completes its flight tests and fitting out, before being handed over to the customer.

The prototype B757 – appropriately registered N757A – was rolled out in Boeing colours on 13 January 1982, and took to the air on its maiden flight on 19 February, powered by RB211-535C engines. By this time the aircraft's order book was growing, as Delta Air Lines had signed a commitment for 60 aircraft. Unsurprisingly, Delta specified Pratt & Whitney engines for its aircraft, and so became the first customer to use the PW2037 powerplant. Anticipated sales to Air Florida and Aloha failed to materialise, although a modest, but nevertheless significant, order for two aircraft came from Monarch Airlines. The company was the first of many British charter operators to select the B757, and today there are more aircraft of this type on the UK register than in the rest of Europe combined.

The first five B757s were used in the flight test and certification programme, with Eastern Airlines becoming the first customer to receive an example of the new Boeing 'twin' on 22 December 1982 – the aircraft entered service with the airline on 1 January 1983. British

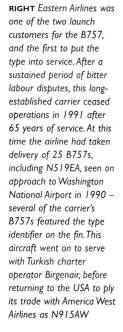

RIGHT Eastern Airlines was one of the two launch customers for the B757, and the first to put the type into service. After a sustained period of bitter labour disputes, this long-established carrier ceased operations in 1991 after 65 years of service. At this time the airline had taken delivery of 25 B757s, including N519EA, seen on approach to Washington National Airport in 1990 – several of the carrier's B757s featured the type identifier on the fin. This aircraft went on to serve with Turkish charter operator Birgenair, before returning to the USA to ply its trade with America West Airlines as N915AW

LEFT *Of the 470 plus 757s operating for US carriers American Airlines (AA) has 98, with a further four on order. AA did not receive its first B757 until July 1989, and uses the type predominantly within the USA, although it is also employed on some South American services. AA has the dubious distinction of being the operator of the first B757 to crash when, on 20 December 1995, N651AW struck Mount San Jose inbound to Cali, Colombia. The aircraft had reportedly 'wandered' off course during the closing stages of a flight from Miami. Realising their error as they descended to land, the crew attempted to pull up over the mountain, but the aircraft stalled when the manoeuvre was attempted with the wing spoilers still engaged. Sadly, all but four of the 167 on board flight AA965 were killed. Sister-ship N649AA is illustrated on approach to Los Angeles in March 1995*

Airways (BA) took delivery of its first machine 24 days later, and the type entered service on 9 February on the Heathrow-Belfast 'shuttle' route. Services from London to Edinburgh, Glasgow and Manchester followed, before the B767 was introduced on European routes, thus signalling the beginning of the end for the Trident in BA service.

The airline operates its aircraft in two different configurations, seating 195 economy passengers on domestic routes and 180 in a two-class fit on European services. It has also used the aircraft on transatlantic routes from both Birmingham and Glasgow. Boeing have made provision for the aircraft to be operated with up to 239 seats in a high-density charter configuration, and several British carriers operate the B757 with 235 seats.

The first flight of a B757 with Pratt & Whitney engines was on 14 March 1984, and that aircraft was later delivered to Delta Air Lines. The 'PW'-powered B757 has since become a favourite of US airlines, and is presently operated in large numbers by American, America West, Continental, Delta, Northwest, TWA, United and US Airways (formerly USAir).

Indeed, the aircraft has sold very well, and operates from every continent except Australasia and, of course, Antarctica – it even services regular routes in the Arctic with Greenlandair. Several Chinese operators have found it an ideal type to supplement their B737s, and China Southwest Airlines uses the aircraft on the Chengdu-Lhasa route. The Tibetan capital is 3542 m (11,621 ft) amsl (above mean sea level), and one of the airline's B757s broke a world record in October 1994 when it landed at the newly-constructed airport of Bangda, in Tibet, which has an elevation of 4334 m (14,219 ft), surpassing La Paz as the world's highest altitude airport.

Boeing introduced the B757-200ER (extended range) variant, with more powerful RB211-535E4 engines each rated at 40,100 lbs of thrust, in 1986. Royal Brunei Airlines was the launch customer for this model, and its first example was delivered on 6 May 1986.

Despite the aircraft having enjoyed a flawless entry into service, Boeing's designers were still working hard to improve the product, and had spoken with several prospective customers for new variants. The first two months of 1988 saw these new models finally announced, with the B757-200PF (Package Freighter) being unveiled in January to coincide with Boeing receiving an order for 30 of the type from United Parcel Service (UPS). This model is devoid of windows and is fitted with a large cargo door in the forward port fuselage. Up to 15 standard cargo pallets can be carried in the main cabin, while there is, of course, additional space below decks in what would be the baggage hold on the passenger variant.

The first UPS aircraft was delivered on 3 September 1988, and the type has since proven so successful that the freight giant's fleet now numbers 73 (with two -200PFs still to be delivered). Miami-based Challenge Air Cargo also has three -200PFs. Outside of the USA, a solitary example can be found serving alongside four passenger variants with Ethiopian Airlines, and the variant has also operated in the past with Zambia Airways.

The second variant to be announced by Boeing in 1988 followed the month after the -200PF, and took the form of the B757-200 Combi – known in Boeing circles as the -200M. Fitted with a forward cargo door, the aircraft can carry up to three containers and 150 passengers. To date, only a solitary Combi has been built, being delivered to Royal Nepal Airlines on 15 September 1988.

Almost eight years would pass before the next new B757 variant was announced – on 2 September 1996 –

by Boeing. The 'stretched' -300 was instantly more successful than the Combi, with German charter operator Condor ordering 12 'straight off the bat' as launch customer for the aircraft.

The main difference between the -200 and the -300 centres primarily around the length of the two types, the latter being 7.11 m (23 ft 4 in) longer. Passenger capacity has therefore increased to 243 in mixed configuration and 289 in charter fit. Cargo volume is also improved by more than 50 per cent. Other changes include strengthened wings and landing gear, and new wheels.

The centre-fuselage section has also been strengthened, whilst higher-rated (43,100 and 43,850 lbs) Rolls-Royce and Pratt & Whitney engines have also been made available to customers. Because of the increased length of the narrow fuselage, the -300 is fitted with a retractable tail skid similar to that employed by both the B767-300 and B777-300. This device helps prevent tail strikes during take-off and landing – an indicator in the cockpit tells crew when such an occurrence takes place.

Aside from the strike indicator, the cockpit avionics as a whole have been drastically overhauled by the manufacturer, with a Pegasus Flight Management System (FMS) installed. An enhanced engine indication and crew alerting system (EICAS) is also standard on the -300, while software options include the future air navigation systems (FANS). Moving further aft, the cabin interior has been modelled on the Next Generation B737, and features new overhead storage bins, with a handrail underneath.

At the 1997 Paris Airshow, Icelandair became the second B757-300 customer with an order for two aircraft. The first -300, destined for Condor, was rolled out at Renton in Boeing house colours on 31 May 1998, and at the event the German airline announced it was ordering another aircraft, taking its total to 13. Arkia Airlines of Israel has also acquired two, taking total orders to 17. The prototype took to the air at Renton on 2 August 1998, several days later than planned, and after a 2-hour 25-minute flight, it landed at nearby Boeing Field.

The first three aircraft (two in Condor livery) were used for the five-and-a-half month long flight test and certification programme in which over 900 flying hours were amassed. This total included several test flights in severe crosswinds at Keflavik, in Iceland, in the aftermath of Hurricane *Mitch*. Joint FAA/JAA certification was received on 27 January 1999, and Condor took delivery of the first two aircraft on 13 March. By the end of this year the airline should have six of these aircraft in service.

In its class, the B757 has proved virtually unsurpassed in fuel efficiency, and can climb higher and faster than any other single aisle twin-jet – it is not uncommon for the aircraft to cruise at 41,000 ft. Because of its impressive performance, the B757 can operate from airports limited

by runway length, high altitude, hot weather and weight restrictions. Its 'baby brother', the B737-400, is unable to service such airports. Due to the thrust available, many operators of Rolls-Royce-powered aircraft use de-rated engines, yet the B757 is still one of the quietest airliners around. The aircraft's ETOPS (Extended Twin OperationS) capability is a boon to those carriers who fly long overwater routes – these include Continental Airlines, and several British and Canadian operators. A refuelling stop does have to be made if severe headwinds are encountered, however. Further reinforcing its intercontinental credentials, the -300 was given a three-hour ETOPS approval *before* it entered service with Condor.

Presently, there are only a small number of B757s in military service. The Argentine and Mexican air forces both operate an aircraft apiece in the government VIP role, while the USAF has also recently taken delivery of four VIP aircraft, which it has designated C-32As.

LEFT *After a period of financial uncertainty in the early 1990s, America West Airlines is now riding strong. Indeed, in February 1999 the airline was the subject of a potential take-over by the giant United Airlines. From its Phoenix base, the airline has seen a steady expansion of its US route network, and its large B737 fleet has been augmented by increasing numbers of Airbus A320s and, more recently, A319s. The carrier's B757 fleet currently stands at 13 aircraft, most of which are painted in special liveries. One of the few which isn't is N913AW, seen clearing the runway at Phoenix in the late afternoon sun. This photograph was taken in 1995, and shows America West Airlines' old livery*

BELOW LEFT *American Trans Air is an Indianapolis based charter carrier with a fleet of B727s, B757s and Lockheed L-1011 TriStar aircraft. Its inventory has grown significantly in recent years, and in the summer months the airline's TriStar and B757s can been seen at many European destinations. The company also undertakes many trooping flights on behalf of the US military. In 1993 the company inaugurated a scheduled service from New York to Riga, in Latvia, using a B757, although this has now been discontinued. Since this shot of B757 N755AT was taken at Phoenix in 1995 the airline has adopted a vibrant new livery which includes a palm tree*

ABOVE *Formed in 1990 as a subsidiary of El Al, North American Airlines operates feeder services from New York's John F Kennedy airport for its parent carrier. Operations began with a single B757, which was later supplemented by a single MD-83. A second B757 has now joined the fleet, as have two new B737-800s. The original B757 – series -23A N757NA – is seen about to land at Los Angeles*

At the time of writing some 966 B757s have been ordered, of which 844 have been delivered. The present boom in aircraft sales may well see the 1000th order for this exceptional aircraft received before the new millennium.

The B757 has proven to be an exceptionally safe aircraft, with only four lost to date. The first occurred in October 1990, and the aircraft was in no way responsible. The B757 in question was operated by the CAAC, and was sitting at the holding point at Guanghzou when it was struck by a landing B737 in which a hijacker had set off explosives. The remaining three B757s were lost in needless crashes in Central and South America in 1995-96.

The first lost was American Airlines B757-223 N651AA, which hit Mount San Jose, in south-west Colombia, on 20 December 1995 when the crew became lost on approach to Cali. The second to crash was Birgenair B767-225 TC-GEN, operated for Alas Nacionales, which was lost on 7 February 1996 when it plunged into the Atlantic off the Domincan coast soon after taking off from Puerto Plata. Faulty instrumentation was blamed for the accident, the aircraft's pitot tubes having become blocked whilst left uncovered during a long ground stop.

The last aircraft to crash was Aero Peru B757-23A N52AW, which plummeted into the Pacific whilst attempting to return to Lima, Peru, following instrument failure at night. This was caused by three of its four static vents being left covered with tape after the aircraft had been washed.

LEFT *Northwest Airlines' N508UA displays the B757's excellent climb performance as it leaves Anchorage*

BELOW LEFT *Resplendent in the early evening sunshine at Toronto is Northwest Airlines B757 N537US. This is one of 48 such aircraft in the airline's fleet, a further 25 of which are presently on order. The first of these was delivered in February 1985 and, until the introduction of the current livery, shown here, the B757s were named after the North American cities they served*

RIGHT *United Airlines did not receive its first B757 until August 1989, although it has since made up for its initial tardiness, and is currently the third largest user of the type with 98 aircraft in service. These machines are employed on domestic services, whilst the larger Boeing 'twins' – B767 and B777 – are used on transatlantic services. Finally, the still larger B747 flies the long-haul transpacific routes. Illustrating United's old livery at Cleveland airport in May 1995 is B757-222 N550UA*

BELOW RIGHT *USAir was also a very late customer for the B757, not receiving its first example until December 1991. A number of these early aircraft were former Eastern Airlines machines, although these have (and still are) since been supplemented by new-build aircraft. Since this photograph of B757-2B7 N615AU was taken at Los Angeles the airline has been renamed US Airways, and introduced a new livery. Six B757s have still to be delivered, which will take the airline's total to 40*

BELOW LEFT *In the last two years the major US carriers have all been reporting near record profits, with one exception – Trans World Airlines (TWA). The troubled company has failed to emulate its competitors, and the fact that the carrier possesses one of the oldest fleets of any US carrier must be a significant factor. Over the next few years, however, that is set to change, as the elderly DC-9s and B727s are scheduled for replacement by Airbus A319s, A330s and B717s. New MD-83s and B757s are also presently being delivered, with 15 of the latter due to supplement the 16 already in service. The introduction of the B757 in July 1996 was very welcome, and although the type is used mainly on domestic routes, it is also utilised on the long New York-Barcelona service. B757-2Q8 N712TW is seen during a rare visit to London/Gatwick whilst substituting for a larger B767. This is just one of three TWA B757s configured for long-range operations*

RIGHT *The most recent US carrier to take delivery of the B757 is Continental Airlines, who initially introduced it on its internal routes in June 1994. Some 36 have so far been delivered to Continental, with orders outstanding for a further five. Three of the aircraft are operated by subsidiary Continental Micronesia, where they have replaced several DC-10-10s. In addition to domestic services, the airline used the B757 to inaugurate transatlantic services from New York/Newark to Birmingham and Glasgow. It is also due to start a new Cleveland-London/Gatwick service in the summer of 1999. B757-224 N17128 was photographed at Kansai airport in Japan in April 1998, operating for Continental Micronesia*

BELOW LEFT *The B757-200PF (Package Freighter) was developed specifically for United Parcel Service, and the freight specialist will soon complete its large order for 75 such aircraft. The airline took delivery of the first example in September 1987 and, along with its B727s, they can been seen at many airports throughout the America. UPS's aircraft generally rest up during the day, becoming active in the late afternoon and throughout the night. Immaculate looking B757-24A(PF) N445UP is seen about to land at Orange County airport in southern California*

RIGHT *Miami-based Challenge Air Cargo recently finally disposed of its last DC-8 freighters, and now operates a fleet of B757s and DC-10s. The Boeing fleet comprises three B757-23A(PF) freighters, the first of which was acquired in 1989 – these aircraft are operated primarily to Central and South America. The aircraft featured here, N573CA 'Spirit of the Caribbean' was previously operated by British carrier Anglo Cargo*

BELOW RIGHT *This photograph of B757 C-FNXY, landing at Gatwick, is interesting in that the aircraft is painted in the hybrid markings of two carriers that no longer exist. The titling and logo of Nationair blend well with the fuselage colours of Ambassador Airways. Ambassador was formed early in 1992 with a pair of 757s, but the aircraft featured here was immediately leased to Nationair. The following winter both of Ambassador's B757s spent the winter in Colombia, where they operated for Avianca. A pair of B737-200s were added to the fleet, but their work lasted just one summer before the airline ceased operations*

BELOW LEFT *Nationair's normal livery is seen here on B757-28A C-GNXC preparing to depart from Glasgow, bound for Toronto. Nationair began operations in 1984 using DC-8s on charter services to the southern US states, the Caribbean and Europe. The airline later commenced scheduled services from London/Gatwick to Hamilton, Ontario, and the fleet expanded with the absorption of aircraft from Quebecair and Odyssey when these carriers ceased operations. Nationair itself folded due to financial problems in 1993. This aircraft now operates for Guyana Airways*

ABOVE RIGHT *Like their European counterparts, Canada's charter airlines have found the B757 an ideal aircraft for their operations. These include transcontinental services, charters to the US, Caribbean and Mexico, and transatlantic flights. In the latter category, Air Transat undertakes frequent transatlantic services during the summer months with its fleet of five B757s and an increasing fleet of L-1011 TriStars. The carrier is also currently in the process of taking delivery of two A330-200s. Taxying for departure from runway 05 at Glasgow is B757-28A C-GTSN. This aircraft previously served with fellow Canadian charter carriers Odyssey and Nationair*

BELOW RIGHT *The operations of Canada 3000 Airlines mirror those of Air Transat, who are its closest competitor. The inventory of Canada 3000 comprises B757s and Airbus A320s and A330s. The airline was the first in the world to take delivery of the long-range A330-200 series, which it uses on its Vancouver-Athens service. The B757 fleet comprises six aircraft, including C-FXOF, captured here on take-off from Gatwick*

LEFT *Montreal-based Royal Aviation added the first of four B757s to its inventory in 1998. Formed in 1991, the airline began operations with B727-200s (one of which it fitted with winglets). Two L-1011 TriStars followed, although in 1998 both examples were leased out, their place taken by Airbus A310s. In 1997 the B737 was added to the inventory thanks to the acquisition of Toronto-based Canair. The airline's first B757, C-GRYK, is illustrated here*

Avianca, Colombia's national carrier, is one of the oldest airlines in South America. Apart from a handful of elderly B727s the airline has a fairly modern fleet, comprising Fokker 50s, MD-83s, B757s and B767s. The latter are used for intercontinental services, whilst the B757s primarily service regional routes. The B757 fleet numbers four aircraft, with leased B757-2YO EI-CEY displaying the carrier's vivid orange and white livery to good effect while on approach to runway 30 at Miami

RIGHT *Aeromexico added the B757 to its fleet in 1993, and the airline currently operates seven of these aircraft alongside four B767s. The airline's sizeable fleet is predominately McDonnell Douglas orientated, with significant numbers of DC-9s and MD-82/83/87/88 twin-jets. The introduction of the B757 has allowed the airline to enhance its regional services, both in terms of capacity and range, with the Boeing 'twin' supplanting other 'MD' jets on services to the US destinations – including Los Angeles, where Aeromexico's N804AM was photographed*

BELOW RIGHT *Aptly demonstrating the B757's exceptional climb performance is British Airways (BA) example G-CPES. This aircraft is one of two which were delivered to London/Gatwick in the spring of 1998 and adorned in the Danish 'Vinger' (Wings) livery. Just over half of the airline's large B757 fleet had been painted in the controversial 'ethnic' livery prior to BA's announcement in June 1999 that the tail designs (by artists from around the world) were being scrapped*

LEFT *LAPA - Lineas Aereas Privadas Argentinas is, as its name suggests, a privately-owned Argentinian carrier. LAPA is the country's second largest airline after national carrier Aerolineas Argentinas. The airline's B737-200 fleet is now being augmented with the B737-700, the first of which was delivered in July 1998. LAPA also has a pair of B757s in service, with LV-WTS illustrated at Buenos Aires' downtown Aeroparque Jorge Newbery airport*

RIGHT *Appropriately adorned in the 'Benyhone' ('Mountain of the Birds') tartan scheme, G-BIKL was photographed taxiing to its gate at Glasgow with snow-covered hills in the background. Prior to the introduction of the new livery, most of the airline's B757s were named after British castles, with Nottingham Castle allocated to 'KL*

BELOW RIGHT *With its main base at Manchester, Air 2000 began operations in 1987 as the in-house airline for the Owners Abroad travel group. The airline quickly earned a reputation for excellence in the British charter business, operating a fleet of B757 aircraft to a number of destinations far and wide. The airline soon expanded operations, with a secondary base at London/Gatwick. Illustrated at that airport is B757-225 G-OOOW, which is a former Eastern Airlines machine*

BELOW LEFT *With the parent company changing its name to First Choice holidays, Air 2000 took the opportunity to re-brand its product, which included a change of livery to a psychedelic red, white and blue tailfin and cheatline. The airline's B757 fleet has recently been reduced to 12 aircraft following the arrival of four A320s. In late 1998 Unijet was taken over by First Choice, and the former's in-house airline Leisure International Airways subsumed into Air 2000. As a result of this merger Air 2000 now also operates Airbus A321s and B767s. Photographed inbound to Gatwick in the current Air 2000 livery is B757-28A G-OOOA*

RIGHT *An Air 2000 B757 leads an American Airlines B767 to the holding point at London/Gatwick*

OPPOSITE TOP
The B757 is the chosen 'tool' for many of the British charter airlines, most of whom operate the aircraft in the maximum configuration fit for 235 passengers. This is somewhat higher than the B757s operated by German carriers Condor and LTU, whose passengers prefer to pay higher fares for more legroom. Many of the British carriers find the B757 ideal for their operations, whether it be on a short hop to Geneva during the winter ski season, or a much longer trip to North America or India. One such operator is Luton-based Monarch Airlines, who undertake the majority of their flights in and out of London/Gatwick – illustrating the point, B757-2T7 G-DAJB was photographed just after take-off from this location. Monarch Airlines' fleet has remained largely unchanged for several years, with six B757s supported by A320s and A300-600Rs. The A320 fleet is presently being reduced in number as the larger A321 comes on-line, and a pair of long-range A330-200s were scheduled for delivery in time for the 1999 summer season

BELOW LEFT *For two consecutive winter seasons Monarch Airlines had a contract with Renaissance Cruises to fly cruise ship passengers between the USA and Athens. This involved a technical stop at London/Gatwick for refuelling and a crew change, where this aircraft was seen wearing Renaissance Cruises titling and colours*

RIGHT *Poised to touch down on the Gatwick runway is Britannia Airways B757-204 G-BYAF. The longest established, and largest, of Britain's charter carriers, Britannia also has its base at Luton, but operates more services out of London/Gatwick than any other airport. The airline has a fleet of 20 B757s, with a further two on order. It has recently acquired Blue Scandinavia of Sweden, which now operates as Britannia AB with five B757s*

BELOW RIGHT *Airtours International has come a long way since it began operations in 1990 with a fleet of MD-83s. The airline's substantial fleet now includes A320 and A321 aircraft, and B757s and B767s – a pair of A330s will also join the fleet in 1999. Expansion has seen Airtours take a controlling stake in Premier of Scandinavia and Air Belgium, with further acquisitions likely. The B757 fleet currently numbers five aircraft, one of which is G-JALC*

MAIN PICTURE
A number of British charter carriers, which have operated the 757, are no longer in existence. This includes Ambassador Airlines whose aircraft G-BUDZ is illustrated

INSET *When one looks back it really is quite incredible just how many British charter operators have been and gone over the past decade. Cardiff based Inter European Airways was the airline for Aspro Holidays and operated Boeing 737s and 757s. In 1993 the airline acquired a pair of A320s, however by the end of that summer Aspro was taken over by Airtours, with the 757s absorbed into that carrier's fleet. Ready for take-off from Gatwick is 757-23A G-IEAB. This aircraft now serves with Airtours as G-LCRC*

Gone but not forgotten! It was a sad day indeed for the British aviation industry when, in March 1991, Air Europe was forced to cease operations due to the financial troubles of its parent company, the International Leisure Group. From its humble beginning as a charter operator, Air Europe had become a major 'player' in the European scheduled service market, and was providing increasing opposition on these routes for British Airways. The airline's fleet was also building rapidly, with B737s, B757s and even a B747 adding to its original fleet of Fokker 100s. The airline's vivid orange and white livery is shown to good effect on B757-236 G-BKRM, photographed against a clear blue skies. This aircraft was only the 14th B757 ever built, and, ironically, was originally intended for British Airways

RIGHT *Unlike their UK and US counterparts, Europe's scheduled carriers have largely ignored the B757's capabilities – not so their charter contemporaries. Spain's Air Europa was a close associate of the unfortunate Air Europe but, unlike the latter, it has managed to remain in business. Its fleet of B737s and B757s are used primarily to convey tourists from northern Europe to Spain's holiday resorts, although some internal scheduled services are also undertaken. Air Europa's livery mirrors that of the now defunct Air Europe, with B757-236 EC-FEF seen on the runway at Luton*

BELOW RIGHT
Air Holland B757-27B PH-AHE decelerates after landing on runway 06 at Amsterdam's Schiphol airport. The airline uses four of the type, alongside a few B737s, on charter services primarily to the Mediterranean and Canary Islands. This aircraft previously served with Danish charter operator Sterling Airways

RIGHT *The bright yellow tails of Condor Flugdienst are a common sight at the airports that serve the many holiday resorts of the Mediterranean and Canary Islands. The German airline has a substantial fleet of 18 B757s, with the first of 13 examples of the larger -300 series just entering service. A small number of A320s complement the B757s, while the larger B767s are used both on medium- and long-range routes. Taxying for departure at Dusseldorf is B757-230 D-ABNM. Condor's B757s are configured for either 207 or 210 seats, which is considerably fewer than the 233- or 235-seat configuration employed by British charter airlines*

OPPOSITE BELOW
Condor has had the fuselage and tail of B757 D-ABNF painted with cartoons that were designed by German schoolchildren, Dubbed the 'Rizzi Bird', it is seen climbing out of Dusseldorf airport, heading for the sunshine of the Canary Islands

LEFT *This head-on view of the aircraft at its gate at Dusseldorf shows off a number of the cartoons to good effect*

ABOVE *Germany's other B757 charter operator is LTU, and, like Condor, has decorated its aircraft in bright vivid colours – this time red and white. Dusseldorf-based Lufttransport Unternehmen has a fleet comprising 11 B757s and six B767s. Some of these were previously operated by the now disbanded Munich-based LTU Sud subsidiary. Looking immaculate as it comes in to land at Lanzarote in January 1999 is recently-delivered B757 D-AMUH*

BELOW RIGHT *Replicating the LTU livery is Spanish subsidiary LTE - Lufttransport Espana. Formed in April 1987, LTE International Airways' fleet comprises just three B757s, all leased from the parent company. Therefore, it is hardly surprising to find that the bulk of the carrier's operations sees it conveying Germans to Spanish holiday resorts – particularly the Canary Islands and Palma de Mallorca. Two of the airline's fleet are seen at the latter location*

LEFT *Spain's national carrier Iberia joined the ranks of B757 operators in June 1993 when it took delivery of its first example. The airline currently flies eight such aircraft, although the airline's B757 operations have expanded during the last year or so due to the trio of Air Europa aircraft operating for Iberia. The company presently has 16 more B757s on order, although these will ultimately replace rather than compliment those currently in use. Iberia has named its B757s after countries from Central and South America, with 'Costa Rica' being allocated to B757-256 EC-FYN, which is seen at Madrid's Barajas airport*

LEFT, CENTRE *During the past decade Turkey has experienced a phenomenal growth in tourism, although many of its charter airlines have enjoyed a relatively brief existence. One which has survived the turmoil that caused many of its counterparts to flounder is Istanbul Airlines. The company operates a relatively modern fleet of B737-400s and B757s, with its B727 fleet slowly being retired. The primary market for Turkish charter airlines is Germany, due in part to the growth in tourism, but also to the substantial population of Turkish workers that live in that country. Photographed at Dusseldorf is B757-236 TC-AJA, which was one of three such aircraft in use during 1998*

BOTTOM LEFT *During the summer of 1998, Turkmenistan Airlines B757 EZ-A012 appeared in Air Alfa titles, for the Turkish carrier had leased the aircraft for a short period to supplement its fleet of A300 and A321 aircraft*

Like a number of other carriers, El Al Israeli Airlines operates only Boeing equipment. This is due to political pressure from the US, and the associated state aid supplied by that country. The B757 entered service with the airline in 1987, and its fleet now numbers nine aircraft. Two of these are operated on lease to Arkia Airlines, who often fly them in an all-white livery, presumably for security reasons. B757-258 4X-EBL is seen in full El Al livery, however, as it prepares to depart London/Gatwick on an Arkia service

RIGHT *Basking in uninterrupted sunshine, B757-258 4X-EBL displays El Al's blue and white livery. The airline's first B737-800 was delivered in February 1999 in the carrier's new livery*

BELOW *Russia's privately owned Transaero Airlines began operations in 1990, utilising a leased fleet of predominantly western aircraft. These included the B737, B757, B767 and DC-10 aircraft. Due to recent financial problems, the airline has curtailed services to a number of destinations and, so as to save leasing costs, reduced the size of its fleet towards the end of 1998. Such was the carrier's problems that only two of the four B737-700s on order were delivered, and at this time their future with the airline is in serious doubt – some of the B757s have also been returned to the lessor. B757-2YO EI-CJY is seen at Bangkok in happier times*

ABOVE *It came as something of a surprise when, in late 1992, Turkmenistan Airlines augmented its large fleet of Soviet-built aircraft with the first of three B737-300s. A year later a VIP-configured B757 joined the fleet. In 1996 two passenger variants of this jetliner, configured for 16 Business and 173 Economy seats, joined the airline. The first of these was EZ-A011, which is seen on approach to London/Heathrow at the end of a flight from Ashkhabad*

RIGHT *Icelandair uses the B757 to supplement its fleet of B737-400s on international routes, and with the recent expansion to its North American network, it has increased its B757 fleet to five aircraft, with a further three on order. The airline is one of just three customers for the larger B757-300, two of which are on order. Seen climbing out of Heathrow, bound for Keflavik, is B757-208 TF-FIJ 'Svandis'*

LEFT *Finnair added the B757 to its inventory in October 1997, utilising the aircraft in an all-economy 219-seat fit exclusively on charter work. This includes flights to Palma and the Canary Islands, as well as further afield to destinations such as Thailand. Four of the five jets on order have been delivered, with OH-LBS displaying the airline's new livery at Lanzarote in January 1999, complete with Santa Claus and reindeer*

BELOW *Seen lowering its undercarriage for a landing at Kangerlussuaq is Greenlandair's sole B757, TF-GRL 'Kunuunnguaq'. This aircraft joined the fleet in 1998 to service both Kangerlussuaq (Sondre Stromfjord) and Narsarsuaq from Copenhagen*

Posing against a typically gin clear Swiss sky, B757-23A HB-IEE is seen devoid of any airline titling. Configured as a luxurious 60-seater, it has been based in Switzerland for over a decade, operating with Privatair (previously known as Petrolair). The company also flies several business jets and a B737-300, whilst two brand new B737 Business Jets are currently on order

RIGHT *Another corporate B757 is VP-CAU, which belonged to the recently deceased millionaire James Goldsmith, and was operated under the guise of Diamond Aviation International*

BELOW LEFT *B757-23A(PF) VH-AWE was photographed at Brussels in August 1996 in full DHL Worldwide Express markings. This aircraft is one of the few B757 Package Freighters not operated by UPS, being ordered originally by Transbrasil, but delivered instead to Zambia Airways, on lease from Ansett Worldwide. The aircraft went on to serve with Gulf Air, before joining its current operator in April 1996*

RIGHT *Ethiopian Airlines has one of the most attractive liveries currently in use, and it adorns its five B757s (one of which is a freighter) and three B767s which undertake international and regional services from Addis Ababa. The aircraft illustrated (ET-AKC) was photographed at London/Gatwick in 1993 while operating the Banjul service on behalf of Air Gambia*

BELOW RIGHT *Air Seychelles was formed in 1979, and soon inaugurated a Mahe-London/Gatwick service with B707s. Later, an A300 was used, prior to the B767s which are presently in use. In March 1993 the airline acquired B757 S7-AAX 'Aride' on lease for use on 'thinner' routes, including a new Madrid service. Unfortunately, during its inaugural visit to the Spanish capital, the aircraft was damaged by a catering truck and had to be flown back to Gatwick for repairs. S7-AAX has since been replaced by another B767*

BELOW LEFT *Royal Brunei Airlines was one of the first Asian operators to buy the B757, taking delivery of three -200s in 1986-87. They have since been replaced on European services by the larger B767, although one is still used on regional routes from the capital, Bandar Seri Begawan. Photographed on a flight to Beijing in 1997 is the airline's sole remaining B757-2M6, V8-RBA – this was also the first example delivered to Royal Brunei Airlines back in 1986*

 गण्डकी

LEFT *The only one of its kind! Rather surprisingly, only one B757-200 Combi has been ordered, and this aircraft has been in service with Royal Nepal Airlines since September 1988. It operates alongside a standard series -200 passenger variant, flying international services from Kathmandu. Named 'Gandaki', the aircraft is seen at London/Gatwick during the airline's twice-weekly service to the Nepalese capital, via Frankfurt*

INSET *Royal Nepal Airlines titling appears in English on the port side of both its B757s, and in Nepalese on the starboard. Note the pennant style Nepalese flag forward of the titling*

RIGHT *The Civil Aviation Administration of China (CAAC) led the importation of large numbers of B757s into the country in the late 1980s. The first few examples of an order for ten such aircraft were delivered to China towards the end of 1987. The following year CAAC ceased to be the only airline in China, reverting instead to its role of aviation and airspace regulator. As a result of this change, a rash of new companies formed – mostly on a regional basis – to operate domestic and regional services. One of those was Beijing-based China National Aviation Corporation, which recently ceased to exist. Illustrated is B757-2Z0 B-2845, which now serves with China Southwest Airlines*

RIGHT *Guangzhou (Canton) based China Southern Airlines Boeing 757 fleet currently numbers an impressive 18 aircraft, one of which, B-2822 prepares to depart Beijing*

LEFT As the name suggests, China Southwest Airlines operates from main bases at Chengdu and Chongqing, in the western portion of the huge country, flying predominately Boeing B737s and B757s. It also has five Tupolev Tu-154M aircraft, but these were grounded following the fatal crash of one on 24 February 1999. The airline has also recently received two long-range A340s. Seen taxying to its gate at Beijing/Capital is B757-2Y0 B-2826

BELOW Shanghai Airlines operates only Boeing equipment in the shape of the B737 (including a newly-delivered B737-700), B757 and B767. The B757 fleet currently numbers seven machines, with a further two on order. B-2810 is illustrated in the carrier's prominent red and white livery

RIGHT *Another Chinese carrier that operates only Boeing equipment is Xiamen Airlines. B737 series -200, -500 and -700 variants are operated alongside five of the larger B757s. B-2829 is one of the latter, and it is featured on approach to Kai Tak*

INSET *The Republic of China (better known as Taiwan) is a very small country indeed. Due to the terrain, and the nation's slow-running rail network, air travel is probably the most widely used form of transport outside of the cities. The short 40-minute flight between Taipei in the north and Kaoshiung is flown some 100 times a day by aircraft like the B737, MD-80, MD-90 and A320. To augment its fleet of smaller jets, Far Eastern Air Transport (FAT) also operates four B757s, with a similar number on order. Photographed as it taxies for departure at Taipei's Sungshan domestic airport is B757-29J B-27005. These aircraft are configured for 209 passengers*

Chapter 2
BOEING 767

BELOW *A name from the past. Piedmont Airlines had an extensive route network throughout the eastern United States, and B767-200(ER) aircraft were acquired for the airline's first international route, Charlotte-London/Gatwick. Their appearance in Piedmont livery at the London terminal was to be rather brief, however, for in 1989 the airline, its network and aircraft were taken over by USAir, which has since become US Airways. Photographed on push-back from gate 37 at Gatwick's South Terminal in 1987 is Piedmont B767-201(ER) N604P. This aircraft was, and still is, a regular visitor to Gatwick as N646US*

Five months after Boeing announced that it would proceed with the B757, the company divulged on 14 July 1978 that it would also be building the B767 thanks to an order for 30 aircraft from United Airlines. Developed simultaneously with the B757, the B767 was aimed primarily at transcontinental routes, as well as intercontinental operations unable to support the larger B747.

Like the B757, the B767 was made available with a choice of engines, namely the General Electric CF6-80 or Pratt & Whitney JT9D, with the Rolls-Royce RB211-524H certified for the later -300ER variant. The twin-aisle B767 normally seats seven across in a 2x3x2 configuration, reduced to 2x2x2 in business class. Final assembly of the B767 is undertaken in a hangar adjoining the B747 assembly plant at Everett.

The initial version was the series -200, and the prototype was rolled out on 4 August 1981. The aircraft performed its maiden flight on 26 September, this milestone taking place five months ahead of the first flight of the B757, despite the latter's head start. By the end of 1981 Boeing had amassed orders for 173 B767-200s, with options for a further 138. The bulk of these orders

had come from US carriers such as American, Delta, TWA and United, as well as Air Canada and Pacific Western from 'north of the border'. Britannia Airways became the first European (as well as the first charter operator) airline to order the type. All told, 128 -200s were built, almost half of which went to US carriers.

The B767-200ER was the next variant unveiled, the extended-range model being announced in January 1983. It featured a higher gross weight and additional centre-section fuel tanks, which significantly increased its range. Ethiopian Airlines was the first customer for the type, its order also making it the first African B767 operator. American and United also quickly swapped some of their orders for the -200 over to the newer variant.

The first B767-200ER flew on 6 March 1984, and in 1986 the type set two new distance records. A Kuwait Airways example on delivery direct to the Middle East from Seattle recorded a distance of 6854 nm, while a Lan-Chile jet flew for 10 hours and 12 minutes on a scheduled service from Rio de Janeiro to Madrid. A total of 101 B767-200ERs were built and delivered in the mid to late 1980s, and it came as a surprise, therefore, when

in late 1998 Continental Airlines bought ten. This was the first order placed for the -200ER for almost a decade.

Jumping forward several years, the only other -200 variant built was the E-767 AWACS (Airborne Warning and Control System) for the Japanese Air Self-Defence Force (JASDF). Based on the -200ER, these aircraft are easily identifiable due to the large rotating radome above the fuselage. The first one flew on 19 October 1994, and it was then despatched to Boeing's Wichita plant for modification work to its electrical power system. Several years then passed before the aircraft were ready for delivery, and for much of that time all four E-767s sat in the Defence Systems compound at Boeing Field. Two aircraft were delivered in March 1998 to Hamamatsu Air Base, where they have undergone a year of operational testing, and the remaining two have just arrived in Japan.

Further military applications for the B767 include its use as a tanker, fitted with both (or either) a flying boom and a hose drum unit (HDU), and as an airborne surveillance testbed – the prototype B767-200 flew in just such a configuration with the US Army for a short time.

In a more recent development for the -200, a number of All Nippon machines have been sold to Airborne Express for conversion to freighters. To make the aircraft suitable for this role, a freight door is fitted and the main cabin floor strengthened. Other freight operators are keeping an eye on the success of the B767 in this role. This mirrors what has happened to older A300s, which are becoming increasingly popular as cargo aircraft.

Going back to 1983, Boeing announced that a stretched version of the B767 (known as the series -300) was to be produced. Two fuselage plugs – one fore and one aft of the wing – increased the length by 6.43 m (21 ft 1 in), allowing up to 37 more passengers to be accommodated. This version had the same maximum all-up weight as the -200ER, and it made its first flight on 30 January 1986. The first three examples were delivered to Japan Airlines the following September, followed closely by aircraft for competitor All Nippon. This variant has received just 107 orders, all but eight of which have been fulfilled. Half of these aircraft have gone to the two Japanese carriers, who use them on domestic services, whilst in the USA, Delta has 26 examples.

The B767-300 was soon followed by the extended range series -300ER, which first flew on 19 December 1986. By far the most popular variant to date, the B767 was introduced on transatlantic routes by launch customer American Airlines in February 1988. The aircraft has also proven successful with Delta Air Lines who, despite having a fleet of 26 B767-300s, also operate 39 ER models – All Nippon also have a small number of ERs in service.

The aircraft has struck a chord with European charter operators too, being used primarily on intercontinental routes due to its excellent range characteristics and seating for up to 327 passengers. This capacity is, however, less than the 361 seats squeezed into the A300-600R in high-density fit.

One of the main attractions of the B767-300ER is its ETOPS capability, which has made it an ideal choice for those carriers who operate the type on long over-water routes. Such is the reliability of modern airliners and engines that the B767 has been instrumental in changing the rules governing such flights by twin-engined aircraft. Previously, such types had to fly circuitous routes that would keep them within one hour's flight of a suitable airport in case of the loss of an engine – a rule that is not applicable to three- and four-engined aircraft. This is, of course, far from ideal from either the airline or passenger's viewpoint, for it increases flying time, and

therefore fuel consumption. However, the reliability of types like the A310, B757 and B767 convinced the various national aviation authorities that this figure should be extended to two hours. This approval was originally restricted to B767s powered by Pratt & Whitney JT9D-7R4s, but it has since been extended to General Electric CF6-80A and Rolls-Royce RB211-535E engines.

There are now a number of airframe/engine combinations and operators approved for ETOPS, many of which are cleared for flights up to three hours from land. These types include the B757 and B777, as well as Airbus products like the A300, A310 and A330. It must be

-300ER, 431 of the type have been ordered and 372 delivered. This compares with just 107 examples of the basic series -300. In February 1999 Britannia Airways took delivery of a -300ER with new Allied Signal Carbenix brakes, which were developed for the B777. All new B767s are now fitted with these brakes, and retrofitting of older aircraft began in March 1999.

The year 1993 saw Boeing announce the B767-300F package freighter, based on the -300ER. It was launched at the request of UPS to compliment its B757PF aircraft, and the carrier initially ordered 30, with options on a further 30. The prototype flew on 20 June 1995, and UPS took delivery of its first example on 12 October that same year. With deliveries now close to completion, none of the options have yet been taken up.

Asiana Airlines also uses a single -300F aircraft, which differs from the UPS variant by having mechanical freight handling on main and lower decks, and airconditioning installed on the main and forward lower decks for the carriage of livestock and perishables. A second aircraft destined for Asiana was not delivered, going instead to Lan-Chile in September 1998. The -300F has a window-less fuselage, a freight door in the forward port side, and a strengthened main deck, undercarriage and internal wing structure. The aircraft can carry up to 24 standard cargo containers.

Production go-ahead of the largest B767 yet – the -400ER – was announced by Boeing in January 1997. It boasts a fuselage stretch of 6.43 m (21 ft 1 in) over the -300 and an impressive 12.86 m (42 ft 2 in) over the series -200. Its increased length allows the carriage of 245 passengers in a three-class cabin, 304 in a two-class fit and 375 in high-density charter configuration.

In addition to the 'stretched' fuselage, one of the jet's most noticeable features is the 2.3 m (7 ft 7 in) raked wing tip extension to improve lift. The cabin interior of the -400ER features some aspects of the B777, including larger overhead stowage bins. Because of the increase in gross weight, the B767-400ER will not match the range of the -300ER and, despite Boeing's press releases, is still a long way off bettering the performance of the A330-200, which is fast becoming a favourite with many airlines.

Launch customer for the -400ER is Delta Air Lines, with an initial order for 21, which has been followed by an order for 26 from Continental. Final assembly of the prototype began at Everett in February 1999, with the roll out in the summer and flight testing to begin in October 1999. The aircraft is due to enter service with Delta in May 2000. Like the B757, Delta Air Lines is the largest operator of the B767 and, as with the B757, American Airlines is not far behind.

At the time of writing orders for all variants of the B767 total 863, with 732 delivered to date.

remembered that each airline also has to prove to the various regulatory bodies that it can comply with all the requirements before dispensation will be granted.

Proving the B767's success as a intercontinental jetliner, both Airtours and Britannia Airways operate across large expanses of water on the London/Gatwick to Auckland route, with refuelling stops in the Middle East and either Bangkok or Singapore. This is quite an achievement, particularly in a high-density charter configuration. There are now also more B767s flying services across the Atlantic than any other aircraft type, although ultimately the B777 could well catch up. To gauge the success of the

LEFT *As with the B757, Delta Air Lines is the world's largest B767 operator, with 91 in use and a further 26 on order (21 of which are for the new -400(ER)). Rumours that the airline will cancel these in favour of more -300ERs are unsubstantiated. The 15 series -200s and 26 series -300s are used on domestic services, while 49 B767-300(ER) aircraft supplement the MD-11 fleet on international routes. For the last two years the MD-11s have operated all services to London/Gatwick, however the B767-300ER took over the Cincinnati service for the 1998/99 winter programme. Photographed operating that route is B767-332(ER) N185DN*

RIGHT *Like the now defunct Pan American World Airways, TWA was one of the great pioneers of transatlantic air travel. The airline is now, however, but a shadow of its former self, for unlike other major US carriers, it continued to lose money well into the 1990s. More recently, TWA has managed to improve its financial situation through the retirement of many of its older aircraft and the scaling down of its operation. Today, the airline's much reduced international services are performed by 12 B767-200(ER)s and four -300(ER)s. One of the former is N606TW, which was looking somewhat worse for wear when photographed at Gatwick in late 1998*

BELOW LEFT *TWA's fleet of -200(ER)s are some of the oldest B767s flying, although their external image has been enhanced by the attractive new livery introduced in 1995. Photographed on rotation from London/Gatwick, bound for St Louis, is B767-231(ER) N605TW, which was delivered to TWA in 1982*

BELOW LEFT *Unlike some of its sister ships, B767-2B7(ER) N653US did not previously serve with Piedmont, having joined USAir direct from Boeing in November 1990. The aircraft is seen here inbound to Los Angeles in USAir livery, and now operates in the black, grey and red colours of US Airways*

*In February 1998 USAir
changed its name to US
Airways, and introduced this
unusual, but stylish, livery
based on a black upper
fuselage. The airline has
recently expanded its
international services, which
now includes a
London/Gatwick route from
Philadelphia. It previously
flew to the London airport
from Charlotte whilst
operating as USAir, but like
many airlines, was duped
by British Airways, who took
over this route themselves
following the short-lived
marriage between the
airlines. The US Airways'
new livery is shown to good
effect on B767-201(ER)
N645US*

RIGHT *Although not quite in the same league as Delta and American when it comes to the size of its B767 fleet, United is nevertheless a large operator of the type – the company flies 11 -200s, eight -200(ER)s and 24 -300(ER)s. The latter have recently taken over some domestic services following the delivery of B777s for United's transtlantic routes. B767-322(ER) N650UA is seen at Rio de Janeiro's Galeao airport in October 1994 still wearing the airline's old livery. United Airlines currently has an outstanding order for ten Boeing B767-300(ER)s which, when delivered, will take its fleet total to 56. Despite the type's replacement on 'choice' transatlantic services by the B777, the smaller B767 is still flying to international destinations on 'thinner' routes*

BELOW LEFT *Based on the B767-300(ER), the -300F freighter was developed in response to a requirement from United Parcel Service. At the time the freight giant was already a large operator of Boeing equipment in the form of 51 B727s, which were being augmented by no less than 75 brand new B757 freighters. The airline placed an order for 30 B767-300Fs, all but three of which have now been delivered. The type is increasingly taking over UPS's international routes from its fleet of veteran DC-8s, and N308UP is featured servicing just such a destination – Sharjah, in the United Arab Emirates*

RIGHT *This May 1989 shot shows B767-233 C-GAUE climbing out of Toronto in Air Canada's old livery. One of the airline's aircraft was involved in a very early safety incident concerning the B767 when, on a transcontinental flight, the aircraft ran out of fuel due to a mix up between kilograms and pounds when being refuelled on the ground. Fortunately, the pilot was ex Royal Canadian Air Force, and he used all his skill to perform a dead-stick landing at disused Gimli Field*

BELOW *Air Canada's B767 fleet comprises nine series -200s and 14 extended range versions. In 1993 the airline added the first of six series -300(ER)s, and these are frequently used on transatlantic routes. Displaying the airline's current livery on approach to London/Heathrow is B767-333(ER) C-FMXC*

LEFT *An Air Canada B767 overflies the Landing Strip on its approach to runway 24L at Toronto. As you might have guessed by the name, this innocuous looking building is in fact a strip club and bar*

RIGHT Despite having operated the DC-10 for many years, Canadian Airlines International uses the B767 on most of its international routes. Early in 1999 the airline unveiled a modified livery featuring a large stylised Canada Goose on the tail, and changed its name simply to Canadian Airlines. Services to the UK are now centred on London/Heathrow, although this shot of B767-375(ER) C-FCAU was taken when Gatwick was used as the London terminus

BELOW RIGHT There are not too many B767s to be found in Central and South America, but Aeromexico uses the type on long-haul services to Europe, although only a handful of destinations are served. B767-284(ER) XA-RVZ is presently enjoying its second period of operations with Aeromexico, having previously served with Lan Chile. The aircraft is seen during a visit to Madrid in November 1998

years absence, Avianca has re-introduced a service from Bogota to London, which currently runs twice weekly, although it is set to rise to three flights per week. The carrier uses three B767-200(ER) and one -300(ER) aircraft on long-haul routes, all of which are on long term leases. The airline's distinctive orange and white livery stands out prominently on N988AN, which is framed by unusually clear December sky while on approach to Heathrow

RIGHT *Lan Chile has been a B767 operator for many years and, in recent times, has added significantly to its fleet, which now numbers 15 such aircraft. Amongst its B767s is a single -300F freighter, although the aircraft seen here, B767-316(ER) CC-CEB, is a standard passenger variant. It was taken on lease from new in July 1996, and was photographed at Los Angeles just two months later*

BELOW RIGHT *Lan Chile has recently introduced a new livery, with dark blue upper and white surface markings being most prominent. The long range of the airline's B767-300(ER)s is crucial due to the geographical location of Chile's capital, Santiago. Because of the relative isolation of its hub, Lan Chile services few European destinations, with, unsurprisingly, Madrid being its chosen venue – a number of other Latin American carriers also fly into the Spanish capital. Displaying Lan Chile's new livery at Madrid is B767-316(ER) CC-CZW*

LEFT *Transbrasil is a newcomer to long-haul international travel, and the carrier's B767s launched services to Europe in 1997 – Amsterdam and London were its chosen 'ports of call'. The company has eight B767-200s, five of which are the long-range ER variant. These are supported by three B767-300(ER) machines, with the latter being instantly recognisable due each jet having different coloured wings! Sadly, this practise has now been discontinued, for early in 1999 the airline introduced a new livery, which also saw a modification to its vibrant tail colours. However, before British enthusiasts had the chance to photograph this scheme, the airline, at very short notice, discontinued its London service due to poor loads. Illustrating the old livery, with its rainbow-coloured tail set against stormy skies at Gatwick, is B767-283(ER) PT-TAJ. This aircraft previously served with SAS as LN-RCC*

RIGHT *Brazil's national carrier Varig has been a B767 operator since 1987, and presently flies six -200(ER)s and an equal number of -300(ER)s. These aircraft are used on domestic, regional and US services, although the type also flies on 'thinner' routes to Europe. In 1997 the airline introduced a new livery of dark blue and white, with the prominent tail logo appearing in a redesigned style in bright yellow. B767-241(ER) PP-VNQ shows the carrier's old livery as it is about to land on Miami's runway 30*

BELOW LEFT *The small island nation of Aruba, in the Netherlands Antilles, has as its national carrier Air Aruba, which was formed in 1988 with the assistance of Air Holland. Initial equipment comprised three NAMC YS-11s, although a direct service to Amsterdam was operated with a B767. In consecutive years three different variants of this type were leased from Air New Zealand, Britannia Airways and Aer Lingus, but the route has since been given up and is now operated by KLM – the airline now operates just two MD-88 aircraft. B767-204(ER) G-BYAA was photographed in May 1992 soon after returning from lease to Air Aruba, and it still bears the airline's colourful livery, but with titling for its owner, Britannia Airways*

RIGHT *The B767 has proven itself with British charter operators, although to not the extent of the B757. Like other such companies, Airtours uses the type predominantly on transatlantic services to Florida and the Caribbean. The carrier acquired two -300(ER) variants in the spring of 1994, and added a third in 1997, whilst two rival A330s will join the fleet in 1999. Photographed soon after delivery, and in full Airtours colours of the day, is B767-31K(ER) G-SJMC*

BELOW *Like the B757, British charter carriers operate their B767s in high-density fit, usually with 326 seats. Their German counterparts, on the other hand, seat around 276 in the same space simply because Germans generally do not mind paying more for better conditions and service. Featuring the current Airtours livery, B767-31K(ER) G-DIMB is seen rotating from Gatwick's runway bound for Sanford, in Florida. During the height of summer, four or five charter flights a day leave Gatwick bound for Sanford or Orlando, all to see Mickey Mouse and his compatriots. In addition, British Airways and Virgin B747s also operate at least three 'schedules' a day to Orlando*

LEFT *A Britannia Airways B767-300(ER) leaves Gatwick, bound for sunny Florida. Note the 'Keep Duty Free' logo on the rear fuselage, which is the carrier's message/plea to European politicians who have decided to dispense with this perk within Europe. This ruling will severely affect not just Europe's charter airlines, but also many airports, which gain vital revenue from this source*

RIGHT *Despite having its headquarters at Luton, Britannia Airways operates far more flights out of London/Gatwick than from any other airport. Its impressive B757 fleet has been increasingly augmented by an ever larger number of B767s. This example (B767-204(ER) G-BOPB), named 'Captain Sir Ross Smith', is seen awaiting take-off clearance from the London airport, with a colleague further down the queue behind it. Gatwick is probably the busiest single runway international airport in the world, with some 800 movements a day during the peak summer months. Although it has a parallel runway, it is too close to the main runway to be used, and is therefore employed only when the main runway is closed due to an incident, or for routine night maintenance*

The name Britannia Airways
came about when, in 1964,
it acquired Bristol
Britannias to replace the
Constellations it then
operated under the name
Euravia. The airline has
since earned an enviable
reputation for service in the
charter business, and has
been voted 'Number One'
charter carrier many times
over by its passengers. The
airline was the first in
Europe to operate the
B737, and its current all-
Boeing fleet comprises
B757s and B767s. The
latter includes six
-200(ER)s and seven
-300(ER)s, with an eighth
on order. Illustrated is
B767-304(ER) G-OBYB.
Britannia Airways also
previously operated six
B767-200s, although these
have now been disposed of

LEFT *Britannia's -200(ER)s
are employed on a variety
of routes, from long
transatlantic services to
one-hour hops to ski
destinations like Geneva
and Lyon. Extended Range
B767-204(ER) G-BYAB is
captured on film about to
rotate from Gatwick*

British Airways acquired the first of a batch of 25 B767-300(ER)s in February 1990, and this fleet was 'topped up' with a further three new aircraft in 1998. All but six of these are based at London/Heathrow, where they are used mainly on European services – particularly since the larger B777 has taken over Middle East routes. The Heathrow-based aircraft are operated in a two-class 252-seat configuration. Named after European cities, G-BNWO 'City of Barcelona' poses in the carrier's old livery

RIGHT *British Airways bases one B767-300(ER) at Manchester, from where it operates to New York, often via Glasgow. Unlike its sister ships, this aircraft (G-BNWH) operates in a three-class F10C42Y141 configuration. That is 'airline speak' for 10 First, 42 Business and 141 Economy seats. 'Whisky Hotel' was the only B767 that appeared in BA's interim livery, prior to the announcement of the recently-abandoned World Images theme*

BELOW RIGHT *The remaining five aircraft in BA's B767-300(ER) fleet are London/Gatwick-based and, again, are configured differently from their counterparts. They boast a two-class 213-seat layout, and are used on transatlantic services to some of the many US destinations served from this London airport. Few people realise that BA operates to more destinations from Gatwick than it does from Heathrow. Furthermore, you can fly to more US destinations from Gatwick than from London's 'primary' airport. Displaying the 'Chelsea Rose' image, Gatwick based B767-336(ER) G-BNWR is seen on take-off at the start of a flight to Pittsburgh*

RIGHT *Some will say 'Virgin haven't operated B767s', but as this photograph proves, oh yes they have! Early in 1997 Martinair B767-31A(ER) PH-MCG was painted in full Virgin Atlantic livery and employed on the Manchester-Orlando service when planned maintenance on Virgin aircraft found the airline short of capacity*

BELOW RIGHT *Air France became a B767 operator by default thanks to its take-over of Aeromaritime. This resulted in all four of that carrier's -200(ER)s, and the first two of a batch of -300(ER), being taken on charge. The -200(ER) is no longer in the Air France inventory, however, for the last two (following several years on lease to Balkan Bulgarian) have just been acquired by El Al. The five B767-300(ER)s are still part of the fleet, however, being used mainly on 'thinner' transatlantic routes. F-GHGH was photographed moments after take-off from runway 24R at Toronto's Lester B Pearson airport in June 1994*

LEFT *Condor Flugdienst is Germany's largest charter carrier, and as such it operates a sizeable fleet of B757s and B767s – although A320s have recently joined the inventory as well. The airline's B767 fleet comprises nine series -300(ER) aircraft, and these are used primarily on long-distance flights across the globe. Unusually for a charter carrier, these aircraft are operated in a two-class 269-seat configuration. Photographed against threatening Alaskan skies, Condor B767-330(ER) D-ABUB is seen about to land on runway 14 at Anchorage*

ABOVE The other German B767 charter operator is LTU - Lufttransport Unternehmen. With main bases at Dusseldorf and Munich, the airline operates a predominantly Boeing fleet of B757s and B767s to a variety of holiday destinations. The airline also operated MD-11s until late 1998, when replacement A330s allowed the 'MD' jetliners to be sold to Swissair. Illustrated at its Dusseldorf base in the carrier's prominent red and white livery is B767-3G5(ER) D-AMUR

LEFT *Over the past 15 years KLM has slowly shifted allegiance from McDonnell Douglas to Boeing (although the former is now, of course, part of the Boeing 'empire' in any case). The airline operates examples of the B737, B747 and B767, and further orders for all three types have recently been placed with the Seattle company. Indeed, the sole McDonnell Douglas type that remains in KLM's inventory is the MD-11. The airline uses its 11 B767-300(ER) aircraft on its services to the Middle East, although the 'big twin' also services the high-density Amsterdam-London/ Heathrow route. The airline has named its B767s after significant bridges from around the world, with 'Rialto Bridge' allocated to B767-306(ER) PH-BZE, seen here taxying for departure at Heathrow*

BELOW LEFT *A partial subsidiary of KLM, Martinair uses its fleet of long-haul aircraft primarily on international charter work – sometimes on behalf of its parent company. Its aircraft are configured for various roles, with only its six B767-300(ER)s fitted out exclusively for passengers (272 of them to be exact, in a two-class arrangement). Its remaining types (a solitary MD-11 freighter and four Combis, plus two similarly-configured B747-200Cs and a single -200F) operate in either the cargo or passenger roles, depending on the route and time of year. Eight-year-old B767-31A(ER) PH-MCI 'Prins Pieter Christiaan' was photographed seconds after taking off from its Amsterdam/Schiphol base*

RIGHT *The B767 has proven to be a popular type with the charter airlines of western Europe, although only in moderate numbers. A typical example is Belgian company Sobelair, which is the charter subsidiary of national carrier Sabena. It operates an all-Boeing fleet of B737s and B767s, with just two examples of the latter jet presently in use (both -300(ER)s). Both are used in a one-class configuration on long-haul routes. The Sobelair livery is identical to that of its parent company, but with additional Sobelair titles. B767-33A(ER) OO-SBY was photographed at Sabena's Brussels maintenance facility*

BELOW RIGHT *After years of competing against the national carrier, Lauda Air now co-operates fully with Austrian Airlines. Canadair Regional Jets and B737s operate European services, and larger B767s and B777s are utilised on long-haul routes, including the service to Australia. The B767 fleet now numbers six aircraft, with a further example on order. Photographed in 1997 when it carried additional 'Partner of Lufthansa' titles, B767-33A(ER) OE-LAS is named after the late Formula One racing driver Ayrton Senna*

SAS - Scandinavian Airlines System has been operating the B767 for many years now, having found the type ideal for its route network, in place of the B747, which proved too large. The airline no longer operates the series -200, however, but it does have 14 series -300(ER) aircraft still in its inventory. These are utilised in at least four different configurations, which match the carrier's needs on its extensive route network. Some are in a 'Polar Fit', with additional emergency and survival equipment for flights which route over the North Pole. Aircraft that operate from Copenhagen to Kangerlussuaq/Sondre Stromfjord, in Greenland, are maintained in such a fit, and B767-3YO(ER) SE-DKY 'Idun Viking' is seen at the gateway to Greenland in May 1996

RIGHT *Spanair was set up in 1987, in association with SAS, in order to capture a share of the charter business which conveyed tourists from northern Europe to the Spanish holiday resorts. Initially equipped with a large fleet of MD-83s, the airline has recently increased its capacity with the acquisition of two former Transwede MD-87s. Spanair also seems poised to order a large number of A320s to eventually replace its entire fleet of 'MDs'. For long-haul routes two B767-300(ER) aircraft have been in use since 1991, these being named 'Baleares' and 'Canarias' in honour of them being the most popular destinations for Scandinavian tourists. The latter aircraft is B767-3YO(ER) EC-FHA, which was photographed at Gatwick in weather conditions which I'm sure the passengers hoped would not be awaiting them upon their arrival in the Canary Islands*

BELOW LEFT *Spanish charter airlines have not been slow to capitalise on the increasing numbers of northern Europeans who flock to their shores every summer, and in the case of the Canary Islands, all year round. Over the past few decades several carriers have come and gone, but Air Europa is now in its 13th year of operation. The airline has an all Boeing fleet of B737s, B757s and B767s, with the latter type being the most recent addition – five aircraft of three different variants are used, with at least one of the three -300(ER)s operating in Iberia colours on behalf of that carrier. Single examples of the series -200 and -200(ER) complete the fleet, with the latter – EC-GHM – bearing the name 'Palma de Mallorca' on the nose*

RIGHT *Formed in late 1989, Air Europe (Italy) was initially a member of the Airlines of Europe Group. Despite the demise of UK-based sister-company Air Europe, the Italian counterpart managed to remain in business. Initial equipment comprised B757s, but these have since been disposed of in favour of the larger B767-300(ER). Two of these were initially leased from SAS, but they have since been returned in favour of six such aircraft operating on lease from the major lessors. All six aircraft carry Irish registrations, with B767-330(ER) EI-CIY illustrated*

BELOW RIGHT *Alitalia added the B767-300(ER) to its inventory in January 1995 when the first two of six such machines were delivered. At first the type was used on the busy Rome-London service, but they are now used almost exclusively on long-haul routes. The airline's low cost division, Alitalia Team, whose logo is seen on B767-33A I-DEIC 'Alberto Nassetti', operates all of these aircraft. Charter operator Eurofly also uses another two aircraft in Alitalia livery*

Balkan Bulgarian Airlines acquired a pair of B767-27E(ER) aircraft on lease from Air France in the spring of 1992. However, as previously mentioned in this chapter, by early 1999 the French carrier had sold these machines to El Al, leaving Balkan without a long-haul capability. The type had been increasingly used on the Sofia-London route during its latter period of service, and it is seen at Heathrow in full Balkan livery (but still wearing its French registration F-GHED), which included the name 'Pliska'

RIGHT *Polskie Linie Lotnicze - Polish Airlines was one of the first Eastern European operators to introduce the B767. Two series -200(ER) models were delivered in April and May 1989, with a -300(ER) joining the fleet the following year. The latter aircraft was damaged in a heavy landing at Warsaw on 31 December 1993, resulting in an Air New Zealand -200(ER) being leased in its place – this aircraft operated in a hybrid livery. The -300ER was, however, fully repaired, and it has since been joined by three more of the type. Named after the Polish city of Krakow, B767-25D(ER) SP-LOB was photographed during a visit to Bangkok*

BELOW RIGHT *Uzbekistan Airways has a large fleet of over 90 aircraft, some 80+ of which are Soviet-built types. In June 1993 the first western equipment in the form of a pair of A310s was acquired, and these were quickly put to use on some of the airline's more prestigious routes. Boeing managed to get in on the act in October 1996 with a single B757 for government use, while two B767-300(ER) aircraft quickly followed. The larger Boeing machine has replaced the A310 on the Tashkent-London/Heathrow route, and B767-33P(ER) VP-BUZ 'Khiva' is seen on approach to the London airport in August 1998. The aircraft is Bermudan registered due the leasing arrangement entered into by the airline. Aside from its Airbus and Boeing products, Uzbekistan Airways also flies three Avro RJ85s, which were added late in 1997. Like the B757, one of these is used as a government VIP aircraft*

Malev Hungarian Airlines broke with tradition when, in the late 1980s, it acquired western equipment in the shape of a BAe 146 and B737s and B767s. The two new-build B767-27G(ER)s, which joined the fleet in 1993, have been used primarily on transatlantic services. The second of these, HA-LHB, was photographed about to land at New York's John F Kennedy airport in 1994

RIGHT The B767 has not proven overly popular with operators in the Middle East, and Bahrain-based Gulf Air has by far the largest fleet, which numbers 11 aircraft. However, it was once almost twice that size, but over the last couple of years the airline has sold examples to various buyers, including Delta, in an effort to cut costs. Astonishingly, Gulf Air then returned to service several of its ageing, fuel-thirsty, TriStars which had previously been stored – these too have now also been sold off. The surviving B767s are used mainly on international routes alongside A330s and A340s. The airline is also the national carrier of Oman and, until recently, Qatar. Omani-registered B767-3P6(ER) A40-GZ was photographed at Doha, which is the capital of Qatar

BELOW RIGHT Note the moisture streaming over the wings of Gulf Air B767-3P6(ER) A40-GZ as it appears out of the murk and low cloud on its approach to Hong Kong's late-lamented Kai Tak airport

BELOW LEFT *Kuwait Airways was one of the first Middle Eastern customers for the B767, receiving three series -200(ER) aircraft in March/April 1986. When neighbouring Iraq invaded Kuwait early in August 1990, two of these aircraft were captured and flown to Baghdad for use with Iraq Airways. Before this could happen, however, these aircraft were destroyed in a Coalition air attack on Baghdad airport. The third aircraft, 9K-AIA Al-Riggah, has since been sold. It is seen here in happier times at Bangkok in January 1988*

ABOVE RIGHT *At first glance this appears to be a near miss. The reality is that Egyptair B767-366(ER),SU-GAO 'Ramses II' is on final approach to runway 25L at Los Angeles, while the American Eagle Saab 340 in the background is inbound to runway 25R. Egyptair has just two B767s for use on long-haul routes, having disposed of three smaller B767-266(ER) variants in 1996-97*

BELOW RIGHT *The largest type in the Air Algerie inventory is the B767-300, three of which were acquired in 1990. Despite the aircraft's long range, the type is used almost exclusively on the short, but prestigious, Algiers-Paris route. This service is undertaken at least twice a day, although the airline now serves Charles de Gaulle airport instead of Orly. B767-3D6 7T-VJI was photographed at the latter destination in 1992*

LEFT *Air Gabon B767-269(ER) TR-LEJ was photographed whilst making an extremely rare visit to London/Gatwick — this route is usually served by the airline's solitary B747-200B Combi, F-ODJG. The B767 was acquired on lease in November 1996 following service from new with Kuwait Airways as 9K-AIA. Having also flown with Polynesian Airlines, Birgenair and Lan Chile, it left the Air Gabon fleet and was returned to the lessor in January 1999*

ABOVE RIGHT *Air Zimbabwe's long-haul fleet comprises a pair of B767-200(ER) aircraft which joined the airline in 1989-90. These are used primarily to service the European destinations of Frankfurt and London, with the latter visited six times a week. The airline also operates a B767 service to London on behalf of Air Malawi. Illustrated on approach to Gatwick in weather conditions more akin to the airline's Harare base is B767-2NO(ER) Z-WPF 'Chimanimani'*

BELOW RIGHT *Although it has become a major A340 operator, Air Mauritius continues to utilise the two B767-200(ER) aircraft acquired back in 1988, and recently added a leased series -300(ER) to the fleet. Formed in 1967, the airline has steadily expanded its route network, both to the east and west. The Airbus types are used for the bulk of its European routes, with the Boeings utilised on shorter services to Africa. Named 'City of Port Louis' after the capital of Mauritius, B767-23B(ER) taxies to its gate at Jan Smuts airport, Johannesburg*

LEFT *Air Seychelles has been operating a B767-200(ER) since 1989, when the aircraft replaced a leased A300 on services to Frankfurt, London and Paris. In 1993 a new B757 was added to the fleet for use on 'thinner' routes, but this has since been disposed of in favour of a B767-300(ER). That aircraft (series -37D S7-AHM 'Vailee de Mai') has replaced the smaller B767 on most services to London/Gatwick, where the aircraft is seen waiting to depart on a beautiful summer's evening*

ABOVE RIGHT *Over the past two decades the economic boom in Asia has made the region a magnet for sales teams from the world's major aircraft manufacturers – Boeing and, later, Airbus have captured the lion's share of this market. The tiny, but oil rich, state of Brunei has both the B757 and B767 in its inventory, with two and eight examples respectively. Illustrated is B767-33A(ER) V8-RBJ*

BELOW RIGHT *Since Vietnam emerged from its long and tiresome war with the US, the national carrier has changed its name from Hang Khong Vietnam to simply Vietnam Airlines. With this change came the first western airliners in the shape of the A320 and B767-300(ER), examples of which were acquired on lease. The latter type has allowed the airline to expand its network westwards to include Paris, although the type is also used on high-density regional routes, and is no stranger to Hong Kong skies. Vietnam Airlines' B767 fleet now numbers six -300(ER) aircraft, although B767-284(ER) VH-RMA illustrated here is no longer on strength. This aircraft was leased from Ansett and served with the airline for four years between January 1993 and January 1997*

LEFT *China Airlines took delivery of a pair of B767-209 aircraft in December 1982 and June 1983. For several years these machines operated on regional routes alongside A300s in what could be termed an 'unofficial flyoff'. The Airbus type obviously impressed the Taiwanese carrier, for in 1989 both B767s were sold in favour of more A300s. The B767s were in turn sold to Air New Zealand, who have converted them to Extended Range standard. Seen in China Airlines' service in 1987 is B767-209 B-1836*

RIGHT *If this logo looks familiar it is hardly surprising, for Eva Air's tail logo is replicated by many other companies within the massive Evergreen Group, including the large Evergreen Shipping Company*

OPPOSITE TOP *Celebrating its tenth anniversary in 1999, Eva Airways has grown enormously in recent years, and now has a large fleet comprised of B747s, B767s, MD-11 and MD-90s. The airline began international services in 1991 with a pair of B767-300(ER) aircraft, and a further two joined the fleet the following year. When the larger B747 arrived in 1992, Eva used it to displace the B767s on the London service. During the first three months of 1994 the airline took delivery of four B767-25E aircraft, and these are used primarily on both domestic and regional services. Photographed entering the runway at Taipei's Sungshan domestic airport for the short 40-minute hop to Kaoshiung is B767-25E B-16622*

LEFT *The first B767s for the People's Republic of China were delivered in October 1985 to CAAC. The government-run airline remained the exclusive user of the 'twin' in China until 1 July 1988, when that same administration decreed that CAAC should no longer operate as an airline. This was the starting signal for many new carriers to be formed, including Air China, which was designated the national carrier. The CAAC B767s were all transferred to Air China, and that carrier's fleet has since increased in size to include six -200(ER)s and four series -300 aircraft. Illustrated in Air China livery is B767-2J6(ER) B-2551, which was the first B767 to arrive in China some 14 years ago*

Since taking delivery of B777s, China Southern Airlines has dispensed with its six smaller B767-300(ER) aircraft. However, the airline's fleet is still heavily Boeing orientated, with over 50 B737s and B757s in service – although A320s are also currently being delivered. Photographed on the parallel taxyway at Hong Kong's Kai Tak airport is B767-375(ER) B-2564. This aircraft previously served with Canadian Airlines

ABOVE RIGHT *As the name suggests, China Yunnan Airlines is based at Kunming, in the Province of Yunnan. The airline commenced services in 1992 with B737s as Yunnan Airlines, adding the China prefix later. Although the B737 dominates, the fleet also includes three B767-3WO(ER) aircraft, which operate in a 263-seat mixed configuration. B-5001 was photographed taxying to its gate at Beijing in 1996, just weeks after it had been delivered*

BELOW RIGHT *Shanghai Airlines took delivery of its first B767 in July 1994, and currently has three in use, with a further two to follow. This airline is one of a diminishing number of Boeing-only operators in China, utilising seven B757s and two B737s (including a new series -700), as well as the B767s. Shanghai Airlines' distinctive bright red and white livery is well illustrated on B767-36D B-2567, which was caught at the point of rotation from runway 36L at Beijing's Capital airport*

LEFT *When the economic crisis struck Asia in 1998, one of the worst affected countries was the Republic of (South) Korea. Its two major airlines, Asiana and Korean Air, suffered terribly, forcing the former to defer many orders and dispose of several aircraft in a bid to cut costs. The airline will, however, benefit from a recent government decision to award it additional routes, thanks to the continued appalling safety record of Korean Air. Asiana operates all three variants of the B767-300 series, namely the -300, -300(ER) and -300F). Illustrated is B767-38E HL7515*

ABOVE RIGHT *Japan Airlines' association with the B767 goes back to 1985, when three series -200s were taken on charge. These were the only 'small' B767s received by the Asian giant, as just over a year later the airline switched to the larger series -300, 20 of which are now in use. Seen inbound to Hong Kong in Japan Airline's old livery is JA8232, the second of the three B767-246 variants to be delivered*

BELOW LEFT *Japan Airlines uses its B767-300 fleet primarily on domestic services, although some regional routes are also flown. These aircraft are operated in a two-class C16Y254 seating arrangement, and when the one outstanding -300 is delivered later this year, the fleet will number 21 (plus the three smaller -200s). B767-346 JA8398 is seen taxying for departure at Osaka's Itami airport*

RIGHT *All Nippon Airways B767-381 JA8567 leaves a substantial quantity of rubber on the Osaka/Itami main runway. The airline operates the largest B767 fleet outside the USA, and it including examples of the -200, -300 and -300ER within its ranks. These are employed primarily on domestic routes, although the type is also used to service some regional destinations. Like the aircraft illustrated, those used solely on domestic flights can be identified by the lack of English titling. Of the 20 series -200 aircraft on strength, 12 are in the process of being sold to American firm ABX for conversion into freighters*

BELOW RIGHT *Some considerable distance south of Japan lies Australia, where there are two operators of the B767. Ansett Australia Airlines was an early customer for the B767, taking delivery of its first example (VH-RMD, which was only the 24th B767 ever built) on 27 June 1983. The airline presently has eight series -200s in its inventory, plus single examples of the -200(ER) and -300(ER) on lease. Displaying the airline's old livery, which had a tail logo based on the national flag, is B767-277 VH-RMG. This aircraft still serves with the airline today, having been delivered new to Ansett from Boeing on 1 September 1983*

Australian national carrier Qantas is one of Boeing's strongest supporters, and apart from operating four inherited A300s for five years, the carrier's fleet has emanated solely from Seattle. B737s and B767s undertake all domestic services, with the latter supplanting the B747 fleet on international routes. The B767 fleet comprises seven series -200(ER)s and 21 -300(ER)s, with several of the latter operating from the airline's Singapore hub. Last of these aircraft to be delivered was B767-338(ER) VH-OGU, which was the 713th B767 built. It is seen at Beijing in March 1999

ABOVE RIGHT *Across the Tasman Sea from Australia lies idyllic New Zealand. The national carrier has been a B767 operator since 1985, and over the years a number of these aircraft have been leased out, or operated in the markings of other carriers. Three series -200(ER)s and nine -300(ER)s are presently in service. B767-319(ER) ZK-NCE is seen taxying in at Auckland in Air New Zealand's old livery*

BELOW RIGHT *A close (in relative terms) neighbour of New Zealand is the tropical island of Fiji, whose national carrier, Air Pacific (known as Fiji Airways until 1971), have one of the most attractive colour schemes of any airline. From its base at Nadi, the airline, and its modest fleet of Boeings, serve many regional destinations, with its larger B747 going as far afield as Tokyo and Los Angeles. The company presently has just one B767-300(ER) on strength, although another example of this variant is due. The airline previously operated B767-205(ER) DQ-FJA, which is seen here climbing out of Auckland. This aircraft first served with Braathens, before being passed to Varig, Air New Zealand and then Air Pacific. A truly global traveller, it presently serves with TWA as N651TW*

LEFT *Late in 1997 Air New Zealand unveiled a new livery based on a predominantly white fuselage, although the Maori Koru symbol still dominates the tail. This scheme is evident on B767-319(ER) ZK-NCJ, seen taxying for departure at Nagoya, in Japan*

Boeing 757-200

1 Radome
2 Weather radar scanner
3 VOR localiser antenna
4 ILS glideslope antenna
5 Front pressure bulkhead
6 Rudder pedals
7 Windscreen wipers
8 Instrument panel shroud
9 Windscreen panels
10 Cockpit roof systems control panels
11 First officer's seat
12 Centre console
13 Captain's seat
14 Cockpit floor level
15 Crew baggage locker
16 Observer's seat
17 Optional second observer's seat
18 Coat locker
19 Forward galley
20 Cockpit door
21 Wash basin
22 Forward toilet compartment
23 Nose undercarriage wheel bay
24 Nosewheel leg doors
25 Steering jacks
26 Spray deflector
27 Twin nosewheels
28 Taxiing and runway turn-off lamps
29 Forward entry door
30 Cabin attendants' folding seats
31 Closets, port and starboard
32 Overhead stowage bins
33 DABS antennas
34 First-class cabin four-breast seating, 16 seats
35 Cabin window panels
36 Fuselage frame and stringer construction
37 Underfloor radio and electronics compartment
38 Negative pressure relief valves
39 Electronics cooling air ducting
40 Radio racks
41 Forward freight door
42 Curtained cabin divider
43 Tourist-class six-abreast seating, 162 seats
44 Ventral VHF antenna
45 Underfloor freight hold
46 Passenger entry door, port and starboard
47 Door mounted escape chutes
48 Upper VHF ant.
49 Overhead air conditioning distribution ducting
50 LD-W cargo container, (seven in forward hold)
51 Graphite composite wing root fillet
52 Landing lamp
53 Air system recirculating fan
54 Air distribution manifold
55 Conditioned-air risers
56 Wing spar centre-section carry-through
57 Front spar/ fuselage main frame
58 Ventral air conditioning plant, port and starboard
59 Centre section fuel tank
60 Floor beam construction
61 Centre fuselage construction
62 Starboard wing integral fuel tank; total system capacity 9,060 Imp gal (41,185 litres)
63 Dry bay
64 Bleed air system pre-cooler
65 Thrust reverser cascade doors, open
66 Starboard engine nacelle
67 Nacelle pylon
68 Fuel venting channels
69 Fuel system piping
70 Pressure refueling connections
71 Leading edge slat segments
72 Slat drive shaft
73 Guide rails
74 Overwing fuel filler cap
75 Vent surge tank
76 Starboard navigation light (green) and strobe light (white)
77 Tail navigation strobe light (white)
78 Starboard aileron
79 Aileron hydraulic jacks
80 Spoiler sequencing control mechanism
81 Outboard double-slotted flaps, down
82 Flap guide rails
83 Screw jacks
84 Outboard spoilers, open
85 Spoiler hydraulic jacks
86 Inboard flap outer single-sloted segment
87 Inboard spoilers
88 Starboard main undercarriage mounting beam
89 Cabin wall trim panels
90 Rear spar/ fuselage main frame
91 Flap-drive hydraulic motor (electric motor back-up)
92 Port mainwheel bay
93 Pressure floor above wheel bay
94 DF antennas
95 Cabin roof lighting panels
96 Port overhead stowage bins, passenger service units beneath
97 Mid-section toilet compartments (two port, one starboard)

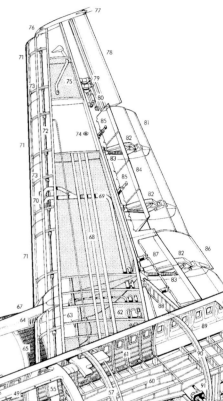

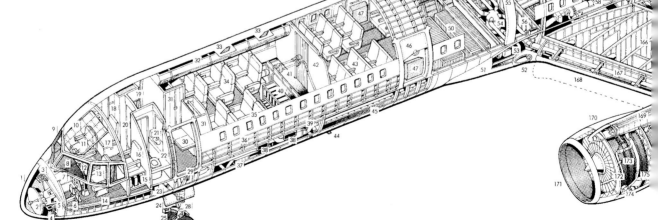

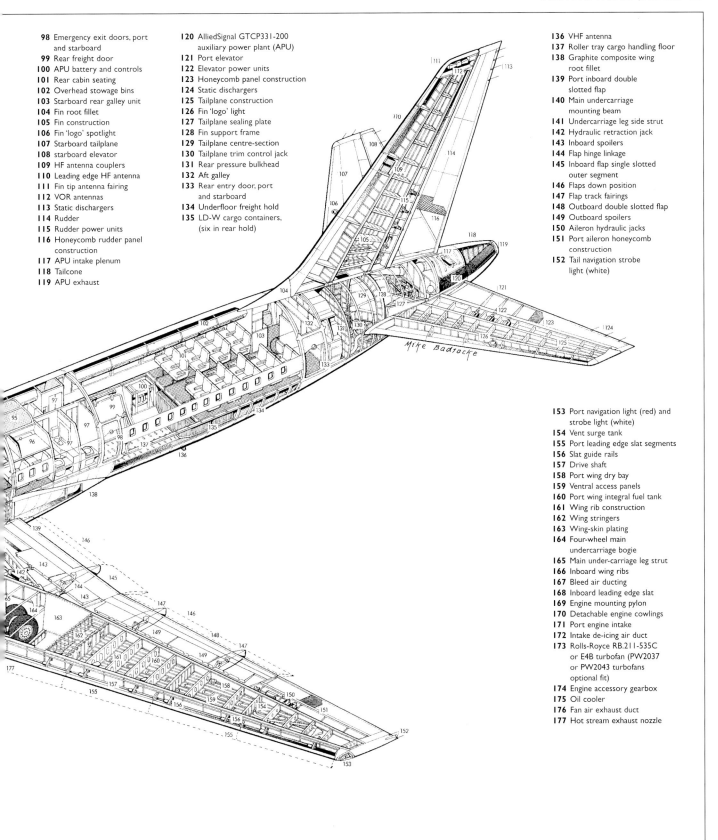

98 Emergency exit doors, port and starboard
99 Rear freight door
100 APU battery and controls
101 Rear cabin seating
102 Overhead stowage bins
103 Starboard rear galley unit
104 Fin root fillet
105 Fin construction
106 Fin 'logo' spotlight
107 Starboard tailplane
108 starboard elevator
109 HF antenna couplers
110 Leading edge HF antenna
111 Fin tip antenna fairing
112 VOR antennas
113 Static dischargers
114 Rudder
115 Rudder power units
116 Honeycomb rudder panel construction
117 APU intake plenum
118 Tailcone
119 APU exhaust

120 AlliedSignal GTCP331-200 auxiliary power plant (APU)
121 Port elevator
122 Elevator power units
123 Honeycomb panel construction
124 Static dischargers
125 Tailplane construction
126 Fin 'logo' light
127 Tailplane sealing plate
128 Fin support frame
129 Tailplane centre-section
130 Tailplane trim control jack
131 Rear pressure bulkhead
132 Aft galley
133 Rear entry door, port and starboard
134 Underfloor freight hold
135 LD-W cargo containers, (six in rear hold)

136 VHF antenna
137 Roller tray cargo handling floor
138 Graphite composite wing root fillet
139 Port inboard double slotted flap
140 Main undercarriage mounting beam
141 Undercarriage leg side strut
142 Hydraulic retraction jack
143 Inboard spoilers
144 Flap hinge linkage
145 Inboard flap single slotted outer segment
146 Flaps down position
147 Flap track fairings
148 Outboard double slotted flap
149 Outboard spoilers
150 Aileron hydraulic jacks
151 Port aileron honeycomb construction
152 Tail navigation strobe light (white)

153 Port navigation light (red) and strobe light (white)
154 Vent surge tank
155 Port leading edge slat segments
156 Slat guide rails
157 Drive shaft
158 Port wing dry bay
159 Ventral access panels
160 Port wing integral fuel tank
161 Wing rib construction
162 Wing stringers
163 Wing-skin plating
164 Four-wheel main undercarriage bogie
165 Main under-carriage leg strut
166 Inboard wing ribs
167 Bleed air ducting
168 Inboard leading edge slat
169 Engine mounting pylon
170 Detachable engine cowlings
171 Port engine intake
172 Intake de-icing air duct
173 Rolls-Royce RB.211-535C or E4B turbofan (PW2037 or PW2043 turbofans optional fit)
174 Engine accessory gearbox
175 Oil cooler
176 Fan air exhaust duct
177 Hot stream exhaust nozzle

Mike Badrocke

Boeing 767-200

1 Radome
2 Radar scanner dish
3 VOR localiser aerial
4 Front pressure bulkhead
5 ILS glideslope aerials
6 Windscreen wipers
7 Windscreen panels
8 Instrument panel shroud
9 Rudder pedals
10 Nose undercarriage wheel bay
11 Cockpit air conditioning duct
12 Captain's seat
13 Opening cockpit side window
14 Centre console
15 copilot's seat
16 Cockpit roof systems control
panels
17 Flight engineer's station
18 Observer's seat
19 Pitot tubes
20 Angle of attack probe
21 Nose undercarriage steering
jacks
22 Twin nosewheels
23 Nosewheel doors
24 Waste system vacuum tank
25 Forward toilet compartment
26 Crew wardrobe
27 Forward galley
28 Starboard overhead sliding
door
29 Entry lobby
30 Cabin divider
31 Port entry door
32 Door control handle
33 Escape chute stowage
34 Underfloor electronics racks
35 Electronics cooling air system
36 Skin heat exchanger
37 Fuselage frame and stringer
construction
38 Cabin window panel
39 Six-abreast first class seating
compartment (18 seats)
40 Overhead stowage bins
41 Curtained cabin divider
42 Sidewall trim panels
43 Negative pressure relief valves
44 Forward freight door
45 Forward underfloor freight
hold
46 LD-2 cargo containers, 12 in
forward hold
47 Centre electronics rack
48 Anti-collision light
49 Cabin roof frames
50 VHF antenna
51 Seven-abreast tourist class
seating (193 seats)

52 Conditioned-air riser
53 Air conditioning distribution
manifolds
54 Wing spar centre section carry
through
55 Floor beam construction
56 Overhead air conditioning
ducting
57 Front spar/ fuselage main frame
58 Starboard emergency exit
window
59 Starboard wing integral fuel
tank; total system capacity
12,955 Imp gal (58,895 litres)
60 Thrust reverser cascade door,
open
61 Starboard engine nacelle
62 Nacelle pylon
63 Fixed portion of leading edge
64 Leading edge slat segments,
open
65 Slat drive shaft
66 Rotary actuators
67 Fuel system piping
68 Fuel venting channels
69 Vent surge tank
70 Starboard navigation light
(green)
71 Anti-collision light (red)
72 Tail navigation strobe light
(white)
73 Static dischargers
74 Starboard outer aileron
75 Aileron hydraulic jacks
76 Single slotted outer flap, down
77 Flap hinge fairings
78 Flap hinge control links
79 Outboard spoilers, open
80 Spoiler hydraulic jacks
81 Rotary actuator
82 Flap drive shaft
83 Aileron hydraulic power units
84 Inboard aileron
85 Inboard double slotted flap,
down
86 Flap hinge control linkage
87 Fuselage centre section
construction
88 Mid-cabin toilet compartments
89 Cabin attendant's folding seat
90 Port emergency exit window
91 Ventral air conditioning plant,
port and starboard
92 Mainwheel doors

93 Door jack
94 Wheel bay pressure bulkhead
95 Starboard wheel bay hydraulic
reservoir
96 Rear spar/ fuselge main frame
97 Pressure floor above starboard
wheel bay
98 Cabin floor panels
99 Seat mounting rails
100 Overhead stowage bins
101 Cabin roof lighting panels
102 Centre stowage bins
103 VOR antennas
104 Fuselage skin planting
105 Negative pressure relief valves
106 Rear freight door
107 Seven-abreast tourist class
seating
108 Rear toilet compartments
109 Cabin attendant's folding seat
110 Rear galleys
111 Overhead sliding door
counterbalance
112 Rear pressure dome
113 Fin root fillet
114 Tailfin construction
115 Fin 'logo' spotlight
116 Starboard tailplane
117 Leading edge HF antenna
118 HF ant. coupler
119 Television ant.
120 Fin tip antenna fairing
121 Tail VOR aerials
122 Static dischargers
123 Rudder
124 Rudder hydraulic jacks
125 Balance weights
126 Rudder honeycomb
construction
127 Tailplane centre section
128 APU intake plenum

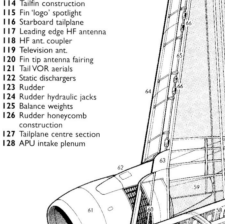

129 Gas turbine auxiliary power unit (APU)
130 Tailcone
131 AFU exhaust
132 Two-segment elevator
133 Elevator power units
134 Honeycomb control surface construction
135 Static dischargers
136 Tailplane construction
137 Fin 'logo' spotlight
138 Tailplane sealing plate
139 Fin attachment frames
140 Tailplane trim control jack
141 Rear fuselage frame and stringer construction
142 Port rear galley unit
143 Curtained cabin divider
144 Door operating handle
145 Rear entry door
146 Pressurization outflow valve
147 Bulk cargo door
148 Rear underfloor freight hold, ten LD-2 containers
149 Air turbine driven hydraulic pump
150 Trailing edge wing roof fillet
151 Inboard flap rotary actuator
152 Inboard double slotted flap

153 Main undercarriage mounting beam
154 Retraction jack
155 Inboard spoilers
156 Flap hinge control link
157 Hinge link fairing
158 Port inner aileron
159 Flap 'down' position
160 Outer single slotted flap
161 Outboard spoilers
162 Flap hinge link fairings
163 Honeycomb control surface construction
164 Port outer aileron
165 Tail navigation strobe light (white)
166 Anti-collision light (red)
167 Port navigation strobe light (white)
168 Rear spar
170 Wing rib construction
171 Front spar
172 Leading edge slat segments
173 Slat guide rails
174 Rotary actuators
175 Slat operating links
176 Pressure refuelling connectors
177 Port wing integral fuel tank
178 Wing stringers
179 Wing skin planting
180 Four-wheel main undercarriage bogie

181 Mainwheel leg
182 Undercarriage leg side struts
183 Port wing dry bay
184 Inboard auxiliary fuel tank
185 Engine bleed air ducting
186 Slat drive motor
187 Landing and taxiing lamps
188 Inboard leading edge slat
189 Slat open position
190 Port engine cowlings
191 Intake de-icing air duct
192 Port engine intake
193 Pratt & Whitney JT9D-7R4 turbofan engine (General Electric CF6-80A or Rb.211-524G/H)
194 Engine mounting pylon
195 Oil tank
196 Fan air exhaust duct
197 Hot stream exhaust nozzle

Mike Badrocke

Appendices

Appendix 1

BOEING B757 OPERATORS (as at 13/3/99)
B757 CUSTOMERS

CUSTOMER	-200	-300
AEROMEXICO	7	-
(Aeromextour)	*	-
(Aeromonterrey)	*	-
AERO PERU	4	-
AWA - AFRICA WEST AIR (6V)		
(loaned from Air Holland when required)	*	-
(Air Alfa)	*	-
(Air Aruba)	*	-
(Air Belgium)	*	-
(Air Berlin)	*	-
AIR EUROPA (some in Iberia colours)	6	-
(Air Europe)	*	-
(Air Europe Italy)	*	-
(Air Gabon)	*	-
AIR HOLLAND	4	-
(Air Madiera)	*	-
(Air Malta)	*	-
(Air New Zealand)	*	-
(Air Seychelles)	*	-
AIRTOURS INTERNATIONAL AIRLINES	5	-
AIR TRANSAT	5	-
(Airways International)	*	-
AIR 2000	12	-
(Alas Nacionales) (operated by Birgenair)	*	-
(Ambassador Airlines)	*	-
AMERICAN AIRLINES	99+3	-
AMERICAN TRANS AIR	8+5	-
AMERICA WEST AIRLINES	13	-
(Anglo Cargo)	* (F)	-
ARGENTINE AIR FORCE	1	-
ARKIA	1	0+2
(Avensa) (joint operation with Panama Air)	*	-
AVIANCA	4	-
(Aviogenex)	*	-
AZERBAIJAN AIRLINES	0+2	-
(Baikal Airlines)	*	-
(BFS International) (Benelux Falcon Service)	*	-
(Birgenair)	*	-
(Blue Scandinavia)	*	-
BRITANNIA AB	5	-
BRITANNIA AIRWAYS	20+2	-
BRITISH AIRWAYS	51+6	-
(CAAC)	*	-
(Caledonian Airways)	*	-
CANADA 3000 AIRLINES	6	-
(Caribbean Airways International)	*	-
CHALLENGE AIR CARGO	3 (F)	-
(China National Aviationn Corporation)	*	-
CHINA SOUTHERN AIRLINES	16	-
CHINA SOUTHWEST AIRLINES	3	-
CHINA XINJIANG AIRLINES	3+1	-
CONDOR	18	2+11
CONTINENTAL AIRLINES	35+3	-
CONTINENTAL MICRONESIA	3	-
DELTA AIRLINES	99+19	-
DHL	1(F)	-
DIAMOND AVIATION INTERNATIONAL	1	-
(Dinar Lineas Aereas)		-
(Eastern Airlines)	*	-
EL AL	9	-
ETHIOPIAN AIRLINES	5 (1F)	-
FAR EASTERN AIR TRANSPORT	6+2	-
FINNAIR	4+1	-
FLYING COLOURS AIRLINES	5+5	-
(Freedom Air International)		-
FREEPORT McMORRAN Inc	1	-
(Gambia Airways) (Operated by Ethiopian)	*	-
GREENLANDAIR	1	-
(Gulf Air/DHL)	* (F)	-
GUYANA AIRWAYS	1	-
(Hispania)	*	-
IBERIA	12+16	-
ICELANDAIR	5+3	0+2
(Inter European Airways)	*	-
ISTANBUL AIRLINES	3	-
KALAIR USA	1	-
KAZAKHSTAN AIRLINES	1	-
(operated for government)		
(Kenya Airways)	*	-
(Kiwi Travel International)	*	-
(Kras Air)	*	-
(Ladeco)	*	-
(Lan Chile)	*	-
LAPA- Lineas Aereas Privadas Argentinas SA	2	-
(Leisure International)	*	-
(Leisure International Airways)	*	-
LTE INTERNATIONAL AIRWAYS	3	-
(LTS)	*	-
LTU	11	-
(LTU Sud International) to LTU 10/97	*	-
(Makung Airlines) to Uni-Air	*	-
MEXICAN AIR FORCE	1	-
MEXICANA	5+1	-
(MGM Grand Air)	*	-
MID EAST JET	1	-
MONARCH AIELINES	6	-
(Myanmar Airways International)	*	-
NASA	1	-
(Nationair)	*	-
(National Air Charter - operated by Zambia Awys)	* (F)	-
NATIONAL AIRLINES	2	-
NORTH AMERICAN AIRLINES	2	-
NORTHWEST AIRLINES	48+25	-
(Nurnburger Flugdienst)	*	-
(Odyssey International)	*	-
(Oman Air)	*	-
(Panama Air International - joint operated with Avensa)	*	-
(Petrolair) to PRIVATAIR	1	-
(Republic Airlines)	*	-
ROYAL AIR MAROC	2	-
ROYAL AVIATION	4	-
ROYAL BRUNEI AIRLINES	2	-
ROYAL NEPAL AIRLINES	2	-
(Ryan International)	*	-
SAUDI PRIVATELY OWNED	1	-
SHANGHAI AIRLINES	7+2	-
(Singapore Airlines)	*	-
(Spanair)	*	-
STAF	1	-
(Sterling Airways)	*	-
(Sunways Airlines)	*	-
(Swiss World Airlines - ceased operations prior to delivery)	-	
TACV-TRANSPORTES AEREOS- de CABO VERDE	1	-
(TAESA)	*	-
(Transaero)	*	-
TRANSAVIA	4	-
(Transwede) to Blue Scandinavia	*	-
TWA	16+15	-
TURKMENISTAN AIRLINES	3	-
(Uni-Air)	*	-
UNITED AIRLINES	98	-
UPS	73+2 (F)	-
USAF (C-32A)	3+1	-
(USAir) to US AIRWAYS	34+6	-
UZBEKISTAN AIRWAYS for Government	1	-
(Venus Airlines)	*	-
VULCAN NORTHWEST Inc	1	-
XIAMEN AIRLINES	5	-
(Yana Air Cargo)	* (F)	-
(Zambia Awys) (operated for NAC)	* (F)	-

Notes
- those listed above in bold capital letters are current operators of type(s) in service
- those in bracketed lower script no longer operate the type, or no longer exist

Present numbers in service (as of 13/3/99)

B757-200	868	763
B757-200M	1	1
B757-200PF	80	78
B757-300	17	2
Total	966	844

Appendix 2

BOEING B767 OPERATORS (as at 13/3/99)

CUSTOMER	-200	-200ER	-300	-300ER	-300F	-400ER
(Aer Lingus)	-	-	-	*	-	-
(Aero Maritime International)	-	*	-	*	-	-
AEROFLOT	-	-	-	2+6	-	-
AEROMEXICO	-	2	-	2+1	-	-
(Aeromonterrey)	-	*	-	-	-	-
(AeroPeru)	*	*	-	-	-	-
AIR ALGERIE	-	-	3	-	-	-
(Air Aruba)	*	*	-	*	-	-
AIRBORNE EXPRESS to						
ABX AIR (N)	4+19 F	-	-	-	-	-
(Air Caledonie International)	-	-	-	*	-	-
AIR CANADA	9	14	-	6	-	-
AIR CHINA	4	-	-	-	-	-
AIR DO - see Hokkaido						
AIR EUROPA	1	1	-	3	-	-
AIR EUROPE ITALY	-	-	-	6	-	-
AIR FRANCE	-	*	-	5	-	-
(Air Gabon)	-	*	-	-	-	-
(Air Holland)	*	-	-	-	-	-
AIR MADAGASCAR	-	-	-	1	-	-
AIR MAURITIUS	-	2	-	1	-	-
AIR NAMIBIA	-	-	-	1	-	-
AIR NEW ZEALAND	-	3	-	9+1	-	-
AIR NIPPON	-	-	-	2	-	-
AIR PACIFIC	-	*	-	1+1	-	-
AIR SEYCHELLES	-	1	-	1	-	-
(Air Tanzania)	-	*	-	-	-	-
AIRTOURS	-	-	-	3	-	-
AIR ZIMBABWE	-	2	-	-	-	-
AIR 2000	-	-	-	2	-	-
(Alas Nacionales)	-	*	-	-	-	-
ALITALIA	-	-	-	8	-	-
ALL NIPPON AIRWAYS	19	-	34	8	-	-
ALLIANCE AIR	-	2	-	-	-	-
AMERICAN AIRLINES	8	22	-	46+3	-	-
ANSETT AUSTRALIA	8	1	-	1	-	-
ASIANA	-	-	8	1+3	1	-
(Australia Asia Airlines)	-	-	-	*	-	-
AVIANCA	-	3	1	-	-	-
BALAIR/CTA	-	-	-	0+2	-	-
(Balkan Bulgarian Airlines)	-	*	-	-	-	-
(Birgenair)	-	*	-	-	-	-
(Blue Scandinavia)	-	-	-	*	-	-
(Braathens)	*	-	-	-	-	-
BRITANNIA	*	6	-	7+1	-	-
BRITANNIA GmbH	-	-	-	2	-	-
BRITANNIA AB	-	-	-	1	-	-
BRITISH AIRWAYS	-	-	-	28	-	-
(CAAC)	-	*	-	-	-	-
CANADIAN AIRLINES	-	-	-	10+4	-	-
CHALLENGAIR	-	-	-	0+1	-	-
(China Airlines)	*	-	-	-	-	-
(China Southern Airlines)	-	-	*	-	-	-
CHINA YUNNAN A/L	-	-	-	3	-	-
CITYBIRD	-	-	-	2	-	-
CONDOR	-	-	-	9	-	-
CONTINENTAL A/L	-	0+10	-	-	-	0+26
DELTA AIRLINES	15	-	26	48+6	-	0+21
(Dinar Lineas Aereas)	*	-	-	-	-	-
EGYPTAIR	-	*	2	-	-	-
EL AL	2	4	-	-	-	-
ETHIOPIAN A/L	-	2	-	1+1	-	-
EUROFLY	-	-	-	2	-	-
(operate in AZ livery)						
EVA AIR	4	-	-	4	-	-
(Garuda) (PK)	-	-	-	*	-	-
GULF AIR	-	-	-	11	-	-
HOKKAIDO INTL AIRLINES-						
AIR DO	-	-	-	1	-	-
IBERIA	-	-	-	2	-	-
(Operated by Air Europa)						
INTERNATIONAL						
EXECUTIVE AIRLINES	-	-	-	0+1	-	-
ITALY FIRST	-	-	-	0+2	-	-
JAPAN AIRLINES	3	-	20+1	-	-	-
JAPAN ASIA AIRWAYS	-	-	3	-	-	-
(Japan Transocean Air)	*	-	-	-	-	-
JAPAN ASDF (E-767)	-	4	-	-	-	-
KALAIR USA	-	1	-	-	-	-
(Kazakhstan Airlines)	-	-	-	CNL	-	-
KLM	-	-	-	11+1	-	-
(Kuwait Airways)	-	*	-	-	-	-
LAN CHILE	-	*	-	14+1	1	-
LAUDA AIR	-	-	-	6+1	-	-
(Lauda Air Spa)	-	-	-	*	-	-
(Leisure Intl Airways)	-	-	-	*	-	-
LUXAIR	-	-	-	0+1	-	-
LINHAS AEREAS de						
MOCAMBIQUE (LAM)	-	1	-	-	-	-
LOT	-	2	-	4	-	-
LTU	-	-	*	6+1	-	-
(LTU Sud Intl Airways)	-	-	-	*	-	-
MALEV	-	-	2	*	-	-
MARTINAIR	-	-	-	6	-	-
MEXICANA	-	-	-	1	-	-
MID EAST JET	-	1	-	-	-	-
(Pacific Western Airlines)	*	-	-	-	-	-
(Piedmont Airlines)	-	*	-	-	-	-
(Polynesian Airlines)	-	*	-	*	-	-
(Pluna)	-	*	-	-	-	-
QANTAS	-	7	-	21	-	-
(Qatar Airways)	-	*	-	-	-	-
REGION AIR	-	-	-	3	-	-
ROYAL BRUNEI A/L	-	*	-	8	-	-
SAS SCANDINAVIAN	*	1	-	14	-	-
SHANGHAI Airlines	-	-	3+2	-	-	-
SKYMARK Airlines	-	-	-	1+1	-	-
SOBELAIR	-	-	-	2	-	-
SOUTH AFRICAN AWYS	-	3	-	-	-	-
(Southwest Airlines)	-	-	*	-	-	-
SPANAIR	-	-	-	2	-	-
SULTAN of BRUNEI	-	-	-	1	-	-
(Swiss World Airways)	-	*	-	-	-	-
TACA INTL AIRLINES	-	1	-	1	-	-
TACV CABO VERDE A/L	-	-	0+1	-	-	-
(TAESA)	-	-	*	-	-	-
TAJIKISTAN						
INERNATIONAL AWYS	-	0+1	-	-	-	-
TAM	-	-	-	0+3	-	-
TRANSAERO	-	0+3	-	1+1	-	-
TRANSBRASIL	3	5	-	3	-	-
TWA	*	12	-	4+1	-	-
UNITED AIRLINES	11	8	-	27+10	-	-
UPS	-	-	-	-	27+2	
(USAir)	-	*	-	-	-	-
USAIRWAYS	-	12	-	-	-	-
UZBEKISTAN AWYS	-	-	-	2	-	-
VARIG	-	6	-	6+6	-	-
VIETNAM AIRLINES	-	*	-	5	-	-
(Virgin Atlantic Airways)	-	-	-	*	-	-
(World Air Network)	-	-	-	*	-	-

Notes

- those listed above in bold capital letters are current operators of type(s) in service
- those in bracketed lower script no longer operate the type, or no longer exist

Present numbers in service (as of 13/3/99)

B767-200	128 ord	128 d/d
B767-200ER	111	101
B767-300	107	99
B767-300ER	432	379
B767-300F	32	30
B767-400ER	54	0
Total	864	737

Appendix 3
SPECIFICATIONS

	B757-200	**B757-300**
First flight	19 February 1982	22 August 1998
Maximum accommodation	239	289
Wing span	38.05 m (124 ft 10 in)	38.05 m (124 ft 10 in)
Length	47.32 m (155 ft 3 in)	54.43 m (178 ft 7 in)
Height	13.56 m (44 ft 6 in)	13.56 m (44 ft 6 in)
Maximum take-off weight	113,295 kg (250,000 lb)	122,472 kg (270,000 lb)
Maximum range with maximum pax	7408 km (4000 nm)	6454 km (3485 nm)

	B767-200	**B767-200ER**
First flight	26 September 1981	6 March 1984
Maximum accommodation	290	290
Wing span	47.57 m (156 ft 1 in)	47.57 m (156 ft 1 in)
Length	48.51 m (159 ft 2 in)	48.51 m (159 ft 2 in)
Height	15.85 m (52 ft 0 in)	15.85 m (52 ft 0 in)
Maximum take-off weight	142,881 kg (315,000 lb)	175,540 kg (387,000 lb)
Maximum range with maximum pax	7135 km (3850 nm)	12,611 km (7836 nm)

	B767-300	**B767-300ER**
First flight	30 January 1986	19 December 1986
Maximum accommodation	327	327
Wing span	47.57 m (156 ft 1 in)	47.57 m (156 ft 1 in)
Length	54.94 m (180 ft 3 in)	54.94 m (180 ft 3 in)
Height	15.85 m (52 ft 0 in)	15.85 m (52 ft 0 in)
Max. take-off weight	175,540 kg (387,000 lb)	184,640 kg (407,000 lb)
Maximum range with maximum pax	7895 km (4260 nm)	11,230 km (6060 nm)

	B767-300F	**B767-400ER**
First flight	20 June 1995	Due 1999
Maximum accommodation	0	375
Wing span	47.57 m (156 ft 1 in)	51.99 m (170 ft 7 in)
Length	54.94 m (180 ft 3 in)	61.37 m (201 ft 4 in)
Height	15.85 m (52 ft 0 in)	15.85 m (52 ft 0 in)
Maximum take-off weight	186,880 kg (412,000 lb)	204,115 kg (450,000 lb)
Maximum range with max load/pax	5556 km (3000 nm)	10,412 km (5622 nm)

Appendix 4
Production Totals (as of 13/3/99)

MODEL	NUMBER ORDERED	NUMBER DELIVERED
B757-200	949	842
B757-300	17	2
B757 total:	**966**	**844**

MODEL	NUMBER ORDERED	NUMBER DELIVERED
B767-200	128	128
B767-200ER	111	101
B767-300	107	99
B767-300ER	432	379
B767-300F	32	30
B767-400ER	54	0
B767 total:	**864**	**737**